Trumpet in Zion

CONTENTS

PROLOGUE · vii

PREFACE · ix

1 OVERVIEW · 1

2 THE ADVENT SEASON · 3

3 THE CHRISTMAS SEASON · 16

4 THE SEASON OF EPIPHANY · 33

5 THE SEASON OF LENT · 61

6 THE EASTER SEASON · 95

7 PENTECOST AND THE FOLLOWING SEASON · 114

8 ADDITIONAL SERVICES · 184

NOTES · 212

PROLOGUE

Theological reflection on the Scriptures is the work of the people. African American Christians have a deeply rooted tradition of learning, interpreting, reframing, and retelling the biblical story in light of their experiences. We are the people of God who grapple with the meaning of the Scriptures for our daily lives. We recognize that we are created in the image of God, with intelligence, creative powers, and abilities. We have also been mandated by God to give birth to new images, new beings, and new things. For we are a part of God's continuing creation story.

Trumpet In Zion is a new creation that seeks to address God in the voice, verbiage, and expression of African Americans at worship. Being a product of the Church of God, it has been my joy to wrestle with the lectionary passages and discover the shaded nuances, overt distinctions, and direct linkages to myself, my people, and our journey with God. As a pastor-teacher and faithful student of the living Word, I have delighted in looking at the old, old story through my Africentric, womanist eyes. My picture of and reflection on both God and Scripture has changed, grown, enlarged, and encompassed more images over the years, due to my education and experiences in the world.

This work is a new resource with a call to worship, call to confession, prayer of confession, words of assurance, responsive reading based on the Psalter, offertory invitation and praise, benediction, and blessing for each Sunday. (Scriptures follow the *Revised Common Lectionary, Year B.*) There are points where information is offered for the decoration of the altar around certain themes.

Trumpet In Zion is a "read-to-use" handbook for pastors and worship teams. It is an educational tool, offered to Christian educators for use in church school, confirmation, and small group study. It may be adapted for use by hospital and campus ministers in their settings. And *Trumpet In Zion* is a devotional guide for those who use the lectionary in a systematic fashion. Although the work is set for use with the lectionary, Year B, the materials may be used freely by those who do not follow the lec-tionary. All parts of the work are compatible for inspiring and promot-ing personal thoughts to flow from users.

My joy and delight has been the rewriting of the Psalter for use in the African American community. During an Annual Conference Spiritual Formation retreat, we focused on the psalms, with Dr. Sister Nancy Shrank, author of *Psalms Anew*. Her teaching on the laments of David's community resounded in my spirit. As an assignment was given to rewrite a psalm for my life, this work was born. *Trumpet In Zion* is my response to God's call to "Cry loud, spare not, lift up your voice, like a trumpet in Zion. Show my people their transgressions, and the house of Jacob their sin." (Isaiah 58:1) These are written as responsive readings to be both the celebrations and laments of worshiping communities.

I am well aware that the limits of this work are due to the boundaries of my world view, education, and life experiences. However, I offer this volume in memory of the ancestors who spoke to God in their own unique, broken, and colorful language; I offer it in celebration of the churches that I have pastored. These faithful souls have allowed me to "practice" liturgies with them each Sunday and on special occasions. I offer it in hope, for the generations that are to follow. They need a record of our praying for them. They need a chronicle of our journey with God.

Rev. Dr. Linda H. Hollies
Grand Rapids, Michigan

PREFACE

Everybody needs at least one good friend. I'm most thankful that God has given me an assortment of friends in my life. I am now more fully aware that friends come for seasons and for reasons in our lives. Some come to walk with us for only short portions of our journeys. Others come and remain constant in our lives. Some come to give. Others come simply to take. Each one comes with a purpose, to help us grow, develop, and become all God intends. The Rev. Dr. Janet Hopkins was and is a gift in my life. She came. She gave. She taught. She shared. She cheered. She prodded. She challenged. She promoted. She threatened. She promised. She struggled. She celebrated. She survived. She fought the ravages of cancer twice. She died. She lives eternally!

Dr. J was a short, petite dynamo. She had a soft but husky voice that spoke with both power and conviction. She was a United Methodist elder when I was yet in seminary. She appeared unapproachable. She seemed to always be in total control. She was an awesome dresser, always sharp, a trendsetter, never a follower of the "customary and usual." She did not simply pastor in the inner city, but was a community activist, bold, articulate, and relentless in her push for justice and equality. Truth be told, I was afraid to talk with her. She seemed to have it "all together!" Then cancer struck her short frame with a vengeance.

As a "colleague" I mailed cards to let her know that I was praying her strength in "da Lawd." Our relationship grew as she recovered and a sistership was born. We shared the insanity and the joys of being African American females in ordained ministry. We traveled to conferences, shared hotel rooms at continuing education events, shopped and dined out together, often exchanging hopes and fears concerning our adult children. Janet was one of the most creative, resourceful, and encouraging individuals I've ever met. She was able to take "little" and stretch it until it resembled much and more! She was a joy to have around, filled with laughter and faith. We spent nights at each other's homes. We found cards that spoke of our friendship and mailed them across the miles. One card we sent back and forth as we needed to hear the words that said "hold on, it will get better." We went through the doctoral program, at different schools, but during the same time period. The speed dials on our phones worked overtime. We took special pains in selecting birthday and Christmas gifts. As I wrote *Trumpet in Zion, A,* she sent me a figure of a black male playing a trumpet. He sits atop my computer cabinet, reminding me to continue writing our collective visions.

We had eleven years of good times of solid friendship. And, when the cancer returned, we walked that difficult journey together. "Sista-friend" Joyce Wallace and I went to visit, to sing to her, and to release her on the night that she went home to be with God. She was a regal African queen. She had already given me my Christmas present, specially selected, early. It is a plate with three dancing women. It sits among live plants in my home, reminding me that the dance of life, love, friendship, sistaship, and faith goes on!

Janet Hopkins is surely missed. She turns up in notes, memos, cards, and the leaflets of books, bringing a smile to my face. Her name is yet on my speed dial, ringing up her beloved daughter, Enchelle Hopkins-Harris, whom she bequeathed to me as a "daughter-sister-friend." I thank God for every memory of this mighty woman of God. This volume is dedicated to her life of ministry. In her honor, I write today! "Dr. J" is now one of the ancestors! Thanks be unto God for a sista-friend named Janet Hopkins who now awaits me on the other side of time, cheering me to "write the vision and make it plain!"

I began this work while serving as pastor of a primarily Anglo congregation. Our cultural context for ministry certainly impacts our thinking, pondering, planning, and writing. Crosscultural experiences can cause one to long for the sounds, language, and music of "home." Crosscultural appointments will insist that one reflect upon patterns of speech, "home flavored" idioms, and commonly known expressions before speaking them in unfamiliar settings. Crosscultural settings bring a deep hunger for telling our "truth" and getting the record straight where stereotypes and aged racism lingers despite the best "good" intentions. A crosscultural pattern demanded that I rehearse my history, reflect upon my present location while doing ministry that ensures that I never "forget" who I am and the teaching purpose God has for me in whatever my location!

Trumpet B flows from a cauldron of mixed feelings within me. I write for a community I love with a passion. I write while in a community that is seeking to know me better and to deal with their individual and corporate racism. I write from a privileged and wealthy vantage point while two blocks away there is the reality of urban blight, economic devastation, and rampant drug and alcohol abuse. I write while within me there is often the painful question, "How can I sing Zion's songs in Babylon?" I write while wanting to leave and yet knowing that I need to stay. For if I left, who would tell the story of Zion? If I left, who would be the trumpet for those who walk past our building each day, hesitating to enter the "strange" but sacred space?

So I wrote. And I thought. And I remembered. And I pondered. And I prayed. And I considered the story of the ancestors. And I recalled their history with the High God. And I remembered how far God has brought us. And I was reminded of my journey and how I arrived at this spot at this time in my life and ministry. Therefore, I wrote. And I waited in anxious hope. And I waited in expectation. And I waited and wrote in the anticipation that a new story always emerges when we pray. For liturgy is actually a form of serious prayer. *Trumpet in Zion, Year B,* simply calls out the news of what happens when the people of God pray, in faith, believing that God does yet hear us and will answer our petitions! You will discover the use of biblical promises incorporated strongly throughout each liturgy. In this way we are impacted, inspired, and informed by the living Word of God!

Writing can be a solitary event. Yet, there are individuals in my life whom I cannot do without. The list is headed by my husband, Charles H. Hollies, who takes better care of me than I often deserve. My grandson, Giraurd Chase Hollies, is the joy of my life and my inspiration for the days to come. My children are my motivation for leaving what I have learned documented on paper. Gregory Raymond, Grelon Renard, Grian Eunyke and her other children, Germal Chasad and Symphony, will allow me to live in the coming generations. My siblings push, promote, and support me; they are the essence of "family" at its best: sisters, Jacqui Brodie-Davis and Bob; Riene Morris; Regina Pleasant and Arthur; and my brothers, James Adams and Jeannette; Eddie Adams and Onnette; David Adams and Kim; and Robert Adams and Lisa.

I honor a group of sister-friends who nourish my soul: Barbara Jean Vinson, Rev. Vera Jo Edington, Alberta Petrosko, Rev. Daisy Thomas-

Quinney, Rev. Dr. Eleanor Miller, Rev. Beverly Garvin, Rev. Louisa Martin, Rev. Harlene Harden, Rev. Joyce E. Wallace, Rev. Genevieve Brown, Rev. Michelle Cobb, Rev. Dr. Valerie Davis, Rev. Ida Easley, Rev. Carolyn Abrams, Rev. Dr. Linda Boston, Rev. Connie Wilkerson, Rev. Cynthia Stewart, Rev. LaSandra Dolberry, and Rev. Carolyn Wilkins. Each of these women counsels, prays with and for, challenges, and loves me so that writing flows, preaching continues, and my spirit is renewed. I count each one of these women as blessings, gifts, and treasures in my life. Then there are my brother-friends, whose love uplifts me and makes me more secure in my position in the family of God. Rev. Anthony Earl, Rev. Dr. Michael Carson, Rev. Donald Guest, Rev. Dr. Zawdie Abiade, my friend Eric Thornsen, and our adopted son, Rev. Dr. Dennis Robinson, accept me fully as they uphold my life and ministry in their gentle hands. Without them, my life would be so incomplete. But, because of them, I am more wholly alive in the body of Christ.

Writing broadens my community. For now you have become a part of my world! I pray that this work will stimulate you to begin painting your own canvas with wide, happy, and life-changing strokes. One of my seminary professors and friend, Dr. Emma Justes, taught me that the Bible not only speaks to us, but speaks about us, individually! Every one of us can encounter our God and ourselves anew, as we read and reflect upon the living Word. May the word pictures of your meditative rendezvous with the Scriptures change your world!

Shalom my friends, God's best Shalom!
Sista Linda

1 · OVERVIEW

Liturgy is the work of the people in the life of public worship. Liturgy encompasses the diverse ways that we rehearse our faith story when we gather as a worshiping community. Liturgy is one of the ways we attempt to give voice to our feeble and inarticulate praise of God. Therefore, liturgy must be inclusive. Liturgy must address the traditional manner of prayer. Liturgy must also speak in the common vernacular of the younger people. Liturgy must look backwards to take stock of our multiple histories, our compound cultures, both of Africa and upon the shores of this country. Liturgy must address our rich heritage of struggle, survival, accomplishments, and exploits. And liturgy must also speak to the realities of our current situations in the songs we sing, prayers we pray, and sermons we preach. Liturgy is not stagnant. Liturgy is a live, swiftly moving river that aims at keeping our inarticulate and spoken relationship with God fresh and ever flowing.

This work begins at the beginning of the liturgical year, with Advent season. Advent is that waiting period for the Christ to come afresh into our conscious awareness. It is also the season when we acknowledge the significant contributions of the Christ Child's mother, Mary, and his cousin, John, and John's mother, Elizabeth. For Advent serves as a reminder that for over four hundred years God had been silent in Israel. That blank page between the last chapter of Malachi and the first page of Matthew signifies the time of no new inspiration or revelation from God! God's first words after four hundred years come with the announcement of two boy children who will emerge from the wombs of their pregnant mothers. Advent is a season of waiting for birth. Advent is a season of getting ready, preparing, and seeking a clean, accepting, and hospitable space for the birth. Advent is distinctly separate from Christmas. Advent is about being pregnant and wrestling with what the pregnancy means and deciding how to deal with the coming birth. Advent is the season for the whole family. After all, men struggle with their own issues regarding childbirth. And children ponder what a new sibling means to their place in the family.

From Advent the drama moves to Christmas and the birth of the Christ child. This season moves into Epiphany, with twinkling stars pointing the way to those who are wise. The baptism of Jesus is celebrated as we hurry through the life of the One who journeys with us to Lent

The Lenten season shifts us from celebration to repentance and waiting for the victory of resurrection after death and burial. New life comes again! Easter gives way to Pentecost and the renewing of our spirits through the power of God's Spirit. Then we begin the long walk through the ordinary times, where the color green on the altar reminds us to grow without celebration.

The liturgical seasons carry us through all the stages of the life of Christ, which is replicated over and over again in our own. The play is filled with rich drama, deep yearning, high festive celebrations, betrayal, pathos, sadness, gloom, pain, and, yes, even death. Just as the advertisement for Prego spaghetti sauce claims "It's all in there!" so the story of our Christian heritage contains every element of our lives. May it always be so!

2 · THE ADVENT SEASON

Advent means Mary is pregnant! This is our time to prepare for the Christmas Day birth. The announcement leads us into a season of cleaning up the mangers of our hearts. Advent is our time to wait as we prepare for the arrival of Christ.

The angel comes to the priest who cannot receive the great promise. He is silenced during the wait. The angel goes to a virgin girl who says "Yes" to the great promise. She is silenced as she walks to the home of the priest and his pregnant wife. When the pregnant wife goes to greet the silent virgin, the Holy Spirit descends and singing and dancing begin. Elizabeth is filled with the Holy Spirit. Mary sings Hannah's old song. John the Baptist dances in his mother's womb. And the world waits for the birth!

It's been a long wait since the Hebrew prophets foretold this virgin birth. During these weeks of Advent, as Mary prepares to bring forth her firstborn child, tell the old stories of a faithful God who is a promise keeper. Tell the old stories of how God got silent for more than 400 years and decided to speak to the waiting world through the bellies of two pregnant women. During Advent, tell the old stories of how we wait for new hope, new birth, and new life!

Altar Focus

The idea is to build the altar each week, beginning with a scene that speaks to the congregation about waiting, watching, preparing, and hope. Positioning a glass star to twinkle over an empty shelter, representing a barn, could begin Week One. Week Two, animals might be placed in strategic places. Week Three, an empty manger can be brought center stage, along with different types of shepherds. Week Four, the parental figures of Mary and Joseph can be seen.

On Christmas Eve, an array of angels might be appropriate, along with many different types of candles representing the light that is to come. The infant figure does not appear until Christmas Day. I suggest you place a large loaf of brown bread in the manger. Jesus is the bread of life and was born to die. It is not appropriate for us simply to get misty-eyed over the babe in the manger, without realizing the fullness of his Advent.

A way to include the congregation in the building of the altar and the spirit of anticipation will be to ask them to bring animals, shepherds, and angels from home. After the lighting of the Advent candle, these gifts can be brought forward.

Many churches place poinsettias around the altar for the Christmas Eve worship. They should not detract from the focus of the worship setting. Sufficient room always needs to be left for the sacrament to be placed. Beauty ought never compromise our true and authentic worship!

Hymn of Celebration for Advent

("Mary Had a Little Lamb"[1] Slow beat to the standard melody)
Mary had a little lamb, a little lamb, a little lamb.
Mary had a little lamb and Jesus was his name.
He was born in Bethlehem, in Bethlehem, in Bethlehem.
He was born in Bethlehem, the Son of God by name.
Miracles he came to do, came to do, came to do.
Miracles he came to do, for me and for you.

THE FIRST SUNDAY OF ADVENT
Isaiah 64:1–9
Psalm 80:1–7, 17–19
1 Corinthians 1:3–9
Mark 13:24–37

Call to Worship

Leader: Ivory soap claims to be 99 and ⁴⁴/₁₀₀ percent pure!
People: Have you lost your mind? It's Sunday morning and you're talking about some soap?
Leader: Tide claims it can get the dirt out. Yet both of them are falsely advertising. The dirt in us is sin. There is no outside cleanser.
People: How right you are. We have all sinned. Even our attempts to be clean are like filthy rags. Our hidden sins are eating away at our insides.
Leader: We gather again to have our hearts, minds, spirits, and souls cleansed for the Advent of Christ.
People: O, come let us adore him. He is the Christ of glory, cleanser of our sin.

Lighting of Advent Candle

Today we begin another intentional period of active waiting for the Christ. In this season we will be more alert, more awake, and more keenly aware of the many ways Christ comes to us. I light this candle of hope. May its glow remind us that we are to always be ready for the coming of the Promised One. Shall we pray?

Silent Confession

Words of Assurance

God has made us like pliable clay. Our God is the potter, continuing to mold us into divine images. When we confess and repent, our hidden sins are forgiven. God will not remember them or hold them against us. With our confession, once again, we are the people of God. This is surely good news!

Responsive Reading

Leader: God, we have heard that you are almighty. The rumor has been that you will kick tail, not even bother to take names and completely wipe out the enemies of your people! Yet, it surely feels like, at times, you have forgotten all about us.

People: God, we have been captured, enslaved, misused, and denied basic human rights. What's up with this? Where are you when we so desperately need you ? From the south to the north; from the Midwest to the southeast, we are mocked, scorned, and harassed. Are you angry with us, God? Have you forgotten about us, God? Have you, too, abandoned us, God?

Leader: We have eaten a daily meal of salty tears. We have been the scorn of others for way too long. We are sick and tired of being sick and tired, God. Come and see about us! Let your smiling face be evident in our communities. Come back from wherever you are and let restoration get busy in our neighborhoods.

People: God, give us life. In the ghetto's blighted urban areas, among the city dwellers and even in the suburbs, allow your presence to shine forth like the southern noonday sun. Let your power infuse us and, again, make us the strong people you created "in the beginning." God, restore us again. Shepherd of our souls, save us from destruction. Shine upon us. Only you will receive our thankful praise.

Offertory Invitation

In every way we have received the grace of God in Jesus Christ. We are not lacking in any spiritual gift. Our sharing in this offering is only a small reflection of our gratitude to a lavishly generous God.

Offertory Praise

God you are so faithful unto us! Receive our tithes and offerings as a meager token of our appreciation and stewardship offered back to you. In the name of the One who has come and will come again, we pray.

Commissioning and Blessing

Leader: Go! Be the Living Word in a world awaiting the Christ.

People: We leave to bear the light of Christ symbols, reflecting that he lives in us.

Leader: Go! Be alert and awake in a world yet basically unaware of a second coming.

People: We leave to be living testimonies in the world we shall touch this week.

Leader: Go! Take the light of hope within you. And what I say to one, I say to all: "Keep awake," for Christ has come; Christ is present. And Christ will come again.

All: It is so! Hallelujah and amen.

THE SECOND SUNDAY OF ADVENT

Isaiah 40:1–11
Psalm 85:1–2, 8–13
2 Peter 3:8–15a
Mark 1:1–8

Call to Worship

Leader: The God of the Broken Hearted is present to dispense comfort.
People: We, the people of God who are often broken hearted, come to apply for tender mercy.
Leader: God has spoken! Good news is on the way.
People: We, the people of God who too often hear bad news, long for sounds of peace.
Leader: Grass withers. The flowers fade.
All: Yet the Word of our God lasts to refresh forever!

Candle Lighting

We have come to the mountain of Zion to herald the glad tidings of the Coming One. We lift up our voice with strength as we light this candle of joy. For our God has come. Our God lives. And our God will come again to feed the flock as a shepherd, to gather lambs and carry them gently as a mother sheep. The joy of the Sovereign God is our strength.

Call to Confession

The Sustainer of us all longs to dwell within our hearts, to be in relationship with us and to offer to us the comfort that we need. Our confession allows us to receive all God has for us. Let us pray.

Confession

God, you promised salvation to all who will choose your love. Our intents have not matched our actions. We have failed to live up to your standards. Yet we long for your shalom. Forgive us our sin. Restore us to your divine favor. In the name of the Christ we pray. Amen.

Responsive Reading

Leader: God's smile upon the earth has brought us a new season.
People: The smile of God has lifted our guilt and pardoned our sin.
Leader: We seek an audience with this smiling God.
People: The shalom of God is the fullness of God's smile.
Leader: Salvation is at hand. God's glory dwells in the land.
People: This is a serious love affair between the Smiling God and us.
Leader: Steadfast love and faithfulness have met.
People: Righteousness and peace have kissed.
Leader: Faithfulness is the result.
People: And God smiles.

Offertory Invitation

The message was given. The Messenger has arrived. What we share will allow this precious message of unfailing love to continue winging its way around the world.

Offertory Praise

In accordance with your promise, we await the new heavens and a new earth where righteousness is at home. Until your promise is fulfilled, we offer to you, with thanksgiving, a share of the blessings you have provided.

Benediction

Leader: The beginning of good news is Jesus Christ.
People: The way has been prepared.
Leader: Beloved, strive to be found in the ways of peace.
People: Jesus Christ is the way, the truth, and the light.
All: We leave to proclaim his name. Amen.

THE THIRD SUNDAY OF ADVENT

Isaiah 61:1–4, 8–11
Psalm 126
1 Thessalonians 5:16–24
John 1:6–8, 19–28

Call to Worship

Leader: The Spirit of God is upon me.
People: God has anointed us to bring good news to the oppressed.
Leader: We are to bind up the broken hearted and to proclaim liberty to the captives and release to the prisoners.
People: We are to proclaim the year of God's favor and the day of vengeance of our God.
Leader: We are to comfort all who mourn.
People: For we are called oaks of righteousness and we display the glory of our God.
All: Now our mouth is filled with laughter and our tongues with shouts of joy!

Candle Lighting

Our Sovereign God loves justice and hates robbery and wrongdoing. God has done great things for us and our hearts are filled with rejoicing. May all those who sow in tears reap with shouts of joy. May those who go out weeping, bearing the seed for sowing, come home with shouts of joy. With anticipation, we light this candle of promise.

Responsive Reading

Leader: It's almost too good to be true! God's favor is upon us.
People: The dream of justice continually fills our hearts.
Leader: It has been said that we are in for great times.
People: The tides of fortune are being overturned.
Leader: Those who have been last are moving on up.
People: Restore our fortunes, O God. We await the fruition of the dream.
All: God is doing great things for us. And we are certainly glad.

Offertory Invitation

We are called to rejoice always, to pray without ceasing, and to give thanks in all circumstances, for this is the will of God in Christ Jesus for us. Our sharing in faithful stewardship brings a smile to the face of God. Let's give in the spirit of our generous God.

Offertory Praise

God, you have called us to hold fast to that which is good and to abstain from every form of evil. By your promise-keeping grace we are saved. We offer these, our gifts, in appreciation for all you have given unto us. In the name of Christ we pray. Amen.

Benediction

Leader: May the God of peace sanctify you entirely and may your spirit, soul, and body be kept sound and blameless at the coming of Jesus Christ.
People: The God who has called us is faithful. We are kept by power divine.
All: Thanks be unto God for the gift of salvation! Amen.

THE FOURTH SUNDAY OF ADVENT

2 Samuel 7:1–11, 16
Luke 1:47–55
Romans 16:25–27
Luke 1:26–38

Call to Worship:

People: We gather, yearning for the will and reign of God to come.
Leader: Our souls magnify God with Mary.
People: We gather, seeking the favor of God.
Leader: Our spirits rejoice in our Savior like Mary's.
People: We gather, for the Mighty One has done great things for us.

Candle Lighting

All of Advent has led us to this Sunday of great anticipation. We light this candle of hopeful expectation in the knowledge that Jesus has come and will come again!

Call to Confession

We spend our lives facing complex situations, as did Mary, the mother of Jesus. She teaches us how to face perplexing circumstances. Too often, the tests of our lives cause us to sin. This is our opportunity to confess before the Almighty.

Confession

Savior, you are more than life itself. We pause now to consider the state of the manger of our hearts. Unlike Mary, we have questioned you with many "Why's?" We have whined, griped, and complained. Our willful sin has put a "no room" sign at the door of our hearts. Forgive us. Cleanse us. Come in and abide, we pray, in the name of the One who dared to come and knock.

Words of Assurance

The God who called David also called Mary and has called us. This Ancient of Days has promised to take us from where we were found, make our names great, appoint a place for us, and plant us, that we might live in shalom, undisturbed, from the affliction of the evildoers! This is indeed good news!

Responsive Reading

Leader: The maker of music has a new song for our waiting hearts.
People: Our spirits sing the melody of Mary, who sang with liberty and joy.
Leader: Generations before us have had their choruses of praise.
People: We add a new beat, but the praise remains the same.
Leader: For the Mighty One continues to do great things in our midst.
People: The merciful and benificent God amazes us with indeserved grace and favor.
Leader: Our help comes from the Maker of the Universe.
People: The powerful have been brought low. The least and the last have been lifted.
Leader: The hungry have been fed and the rich turned away from the feast of life.
People: God's memory has never slipped! We are always in the mind of the Helper of the Oppressed.
Leader: The music of the heavenly spheres cannot begin to compare with our combined notes of thanks.
People: Our musicology is limited. But the chords of our praise will ring throughout eternity. Sing, we will. Sing, we shall. Sing, we must! For our souls magnify God!

Offertory Invitation

Mary risked her life to give to God. Elizabeth risked her life to give to God. No less is expected of us. This is our time to express our sacrifice of love. Let's be as generous as our sisters.

Offertory Praise

Great Giver of All, here we are. These gifts represent such a small token of what we have received. For we are so mindful that all we have is a gift from you. Receive now what we have to offer, in the name of the Baby Born to Die.

Benediction

Leader: Now to God, who is able to strengthen us according to the good news of Jesus, according to the revelation of the mystery that has now been disclosed to us through the obedience of our faith, to the only true God, through Jesus Christ, be the glory forever! Amen.
People: It is so!

CHRISTMAS EVE

Isaiah 9:2–7
Psalm 96
Titus 2:11–14
Luke 2:1–14

Call to Worship

Leader: On this night we join with the angelic choir in offering praise to the newborn King.
People: The whole earth offers God a brand new song of eternal thanks.
Leader: A generous God has loved so mightily until Love's descant echos across the world.
People: The splendor of the heavens radiates in each face. Hope is born anew this night.
All: Angels we have heard! Now the angels will listen to our glad songs!

Candle Lighting

The house and realm of God stand sure forever. The throne of God is established forever. The people of God are loved forever. In memory of every promise made and kept for the ancestors, we light this candle of anticipation with eternal joy!

Responsive Reading

Leader: We are called to sing new songs unto God on this most holy of all nights.
People: The elements are joining in this command to offer new songs of praise.
Leader: From sea to shining sea, from mountaintop to valley low, there are sounds of great joy being lifted unto God.
People: God is great and working on our behalf right now.
Leader: We have waited in anticipation for this magnificent event of new birth.
People: We know that God has come and tonight we shout, "Encore, God, encore!"

Leader: The God who has come is present already, even as we wait.
People: We have brought gifts and we have gathered to celebrate before the beauty of this great God who comes again and again.
Leader: The sky is shouting out its praise with bright stars.
People: We bring our voices and the sounds of cheering applause.
Leader: Together we offer extravagant thanks for extravagant Love, which came to earth on Christmas Day.
People: The God who came will come again. This is our certain hope and our excellent praise!

Offertory Invitation

The powerful have been pulled down from their thrones. The hungry have been filled with good things. The rich have been turned away empty. And we have been called to share in order that this upside down story continues.

Offertory Praise

God, nothing is impossible with you. Take these small tokens of our thanksgiving and enlarge them for use in the world we will never reach or see. Magnify them to be used for your glory, world without end. Amen.

Benediction

Leader: Now unto God, who is able to strengthen you according to the rich gospel and proclamation of Jesus Christ, according to the revelation of the mystery that was kept secret for long ages but is now disclosed and made known unto us, to the only wise God through Jesus Christ, be glory and honor forever.
All: Amen!

3 · THE CHRISTMAS SEASON

The Hope of the world is Jesus! We celebrate his moving into our skin, sharing our humanity, and winning for us the victory over death, the grave, and hell. Christmas is not simply one day. Christmas is a season of sharing the mystery of God's love made manifest in Jesus Christ. Christmas is a season of wonder, where the Babe in Bethlehem captures the attention of the whole world. Christmas is the season of new hope, new joy, and a newfound sense of community. May this be a Mary's Christmas for you and your congregation! Look for the angels. Watch for the stars. Prepare for the shepherds. Be in tune with the angelic songs. Open your heart and allow there to be room in the inn of your heart!

Christmas is the season that leads us into Epiphany, where we are urged to be on the lookout for signs of Christ's presence in our midst.

CHRISTMAS DAY · PROPER 1

Isaiah 9:2–7
Psalm 96
Titus 2:11–14
Luke 2:1–20

Call to Worship

Leader: Arise! Shine! Let's give God glory and praise!
People: We who have walked in gloom have experienced a new light.
Jesus Christ the Savior is born!
Leader: Yokes have been broken, the rod of the oppressor is smashed, and slavery is abolished forever!
People: A child has been born, a Son given unto us. Power and authority are invested in him.
Leader: His name is Wonderful Counselor, Mighty God, Everlasting Creator, and Prince of Peace.
People: This God of shalom is our God and Zion will forever worship, in spirit and in truth. Amen.

Lighting the Christ Candle

It's an awesome story, this birth of a babe in Bethlehem. It's been told over and over again. Homeless parents, with no family around, are forced to have their child in a stable, filled with animals and awful smells. The Child of Peace is laid in a manger, signifying that he is food for the hungry and bread in a starving land. This infant was born to die! The stars danced, the angels sang a cantata, and animals bowed low in humble submission, representing us before the lover of our souls. We light this candle today, because we were not there to participate in the birthday party of the Son of the Most High God. But when he comes again, we will be present!

Call to Confession

On this holy day, our hearts need to be the cradle of love, tenderly holding the Savior of the world. Let our confession prepare us for this awesome duty.

Silent Confession

Words of Assurance

For us, Mary had a little Lamb, and Jesus is his name! Thanks be unto God. Amen.

Responsive Reading

Leader: Let's sing unto the Lord a new song!
People: Our God is an awesome God![2]
Leader: Bless the Lord, tell of this great salvation from day to day.
People: What a mighty God we serve![3]
Leader: Declare the Sovereign's glory among the people.
People: Our God reigns![4]
Leader: Great is the Lord, greatly to be praised!
People: Go, tell it upon the mountain![5]
Leader: Honor and Majesty, Strength and Beauty are strong names of God in this sanctuary.
People: Come by here, good Lord![6]
Leader: Give the Power that Saves, glory. Bring an appropriate offering of thanksgiving.
People: What shall I render?[7]
Leader: Simply worship the Lord, in the beauty of holiness. For our God reigns![8]
People: Ain't dat good news![9] Amen!

Offertory Invitation

The grace of God has appeared, bringing salvation to us all. While we have waited for this blessed hope, today is the manifestation of God's abundant and abounding love for us. While we were yet sinners, God loved us and sent Jesus to be born, just to die for us! God has already given unto us. Let us now respond to this glorious gift.

Offertory Praise

Glory to God in the highest and on earth, peace! Thank you, Amazing God, for giving us eternal life in Jesus Christ. May our offerings spread the compassion, the healing, and the work of justice that his coming announced and his ministry proclaimed. Amen!

Benediction

Leader: Joy to the world, the Lord is come![10]
People: We leave to spread this good news.
Leader: Joy to the world, the Lord is in you!
People: Thanks be to God for this immeasurable gift.
Leader: Joy to the world, the Lord will come again!
People: We will proclaim this message in our lives.
Leader: The grace of God and the sweet communion of the Holy Spirit and the love of the Child who came to die, go with you. Alleluia and amen!

CHRISTMAS · PROPER 2

Isaiah 62:6–12
Psalm 97
Titus 3:47
Luke 2:8–20

Call to Worship

Leader: Holy people, redeemed of the Lord, the Christ Child has arrived.
People: Glory, honor, power, and majesty is the praise upon our lips.
Worthy is the Lamb of God!
Leader: Let the earth be glad and the coasts sing with joy.
People: It is a Mary's Christmas. She has been delivered. Jesus is among us.
All: This is a celebration of joyful hearts. Thanks be to God.

Lighting the Christ Candle

Our salvation has come. Our reward for the long wait has arrived. God has sought us in our sin, helped us to clear out the mangers of our hearts, and helped us be ready to receive this visit from Jesus. We light this candle in honor of his arrival.

Call to Confession

The Lord loves those who hate evil. God guards and preserves the faithful. Let the confession of our sin rescue us from the coming judgment of God.

Confession

God, your goodness and kindness have appeared to us in Jesus Christ. Your holy child has put on our flesh and moved into our human community. Let the radiant light of your glory sweep upon our hearts. Forgive our sin. Remove all that is unpleasing to you. Make us worthy mangers for your presence. In the name of Christ we pray. Amen.

Words of Assurance

God's mercy endures to all generations. By the renewing power of the Holy Spirit we are washed clean and made ready to host the Savior. This is good news.

Responsive Reading

Leader: There is a ruler in the hood!
People. We have a need to shout and celebrate.
Leader: The posse of the ruler includes the twins of right living and justice. They ride ahead to clear the way.
People: There is a ruler in the hood!
Leader: The whole earth trembles, even the mountains melt like wax.
People: There is a ruler in the hood!
Leader: Heaven sent the announcement. Things will be put in order.
People: This is a glorious day of victory. There is a ruler in the hood and King Jesus is his name. We his people shout out our praise.

Offertory Invitation

Joseph and Mary gave all they had. It is now required of us that we share in the task of joyous giving. Our giving says we want there to always be room in the inn for the Christ.

Offertory Praise

The power of the Holy Spirit has been poured out so richly upon us in Jesus Christ, our Savior. We give these gifts in thanksgiving that others may become heirs to the hope of eternal life.

Benediction

Leader: The angelic choir has hushed. The shepherds have gone back to work. The manger has been returned to the stable animals. Only our hearts now hold the One who was born to die. Go into the world, telling all that the Savior has indeed been born in you.
People: The shalom of Christ is ours to spread.
All: Thanks be to God!

CHRISTMAS · PROPER 3

Isaiah 52:7–10
Psalm 98
Hebrews 1:1–12
John 1:1–14

Call to Worship

Leader: Step lively! Step lively! God enjoys lively feet.
People: What's up with the feet and the stepping? It's Christmas morning!
Leader: So right you are, my sisters and brothers. How beautiful are the feet of those who will tell the news that our God reigns.
All: With praise upon our lips and rejoicing in our feet, we'll step lively to inform the world that Christ is born in us!

Candle Lighting

The Holy Arm of God is revealed through the birth of Jesus Christ. We light this candle to announce the good news with joy!

Call to Confession

Jesus is the reflection of God's glory and the exact imprint of God's very being. With our confession of sin that holy image is seen in us. Let us pray.

Confession

We fess up! For surely we have messed up. We've spent too much on the material stuff of this holy season. Today we ask forgiveness of the sin that controls us. Cleanse us and sustain by your Living Word. In the name of Jesus Christ we pray.

Words of Assurance

Long ago God spoke to our ancestors in multiple and various ways. On this Christmas Day God speaks to us by the coming of the Beloved Son. This is good news.

Responsive Reading

Leader: Turn up the decibels. Pump up the praise. It's new song time in the house!

People: We have new songs to offer unto God. For new blessings have been received. New mercy has been extended.

Leader: We have the victory! Despite situations and circumstances that appear to the contrary, this day is a shout for victory!

People: The whole earth is glad and filled with melodies of praise.

Leader: The Maestro of Music deserves to be lifted up.

People: We will make a joyful noise unto God. Turn up the decibels, for we are turning up the praise!

Offertory Invitation

The oil of gladness is our gift today. Let our giving reflect our grateful hearts.

Offertory praise

God is the same. God's years will never end. For the constant and faithful gifts we have received, we offer back a portion in thanks. To God be the glory. Amen.

Benediction

Leader: The Word is flesh.

People: The Word came to us.

Leader: The Word is flesh.

People: The Word lives among us.

Leader: The Word is flesh.

People: The Word lives in us.

Leader: Go! Be living testimonies that Jesus is alive forevermore!

All: We leave in the power of the Living Word. Amen.

THE FIRST SUNDAY AFTER CHRISTMAS

Isaiah 61:10–62:3
Psalm 148
Galatians 4:4–7
Luke 2:22–40

Call to Worship

Leader: This is our day of great rejoicing!
People: We have gathered to celebrate our God.
Leader: God has clothed us with the garments of salvation.
People: We have been covered with robes of righteousness.
Leader: We are like a bride and a groom on their wedding day.
People: We worship because our love for God springs forth as praise. The Beloved Son has come. We have come to celebrate!

Lighting the Christ Candle

The fullness of time has arrived! God's only son, Jesus, has been born of Mary, according to the Law. We have been adopted! We are not slaves! We are royal heirs to all that belongs to God! We light this candle to honor the Christ whose divinity we now possess. The promise has been fulfilled. We are free! We are the children of the Most High God.

Call to Confession

Brothers and sisters, we live in a period of time where those of dark hue are suspect, reviled, mistreated, and even killed. The treatment of others too often impacts the ways in which we think and act toward each other. The time of confession calls us to see ouselves as God sees us. Let us confess our sin.

Silent Confession

Words of Assurance

Jesus has come, calling us by a new name. Jesus has come with crowns of beauty and royal diadems for a regal people. Our confession makes us ready to reign as royal subjects of a loving and vindicating God. This is indeed good news!

Responsive Readings

Leader: Praise God! Praise the abundant God.

People: For a bountiful harvest and the celebration of first fruits, we give God praise.

Leader: For the power of community and its call to unity, let's give God praise.

People: Our God created the first garden, gave it to the ancestors, and charged them to be fruitful and to multiply. We are their heritage.

Leader: For community and the gift of each other, our God is worthy of praise.

People: Every mountain, hill, cedar, oak, wild animal, cattle, creeping and flying thing is a gift to be cherished and preserved.

Leader: Young men and women, elders and seasoned ones, self-determination, perseverance, and purpose are in our hands.

People: Bring the mat, light the menorah, and lift up the cup of salvation. As we honor the past and plan for the future, remember the High God who has raised a cornucopia of treasures for us in our present times.

Leader: People of the Diaspora, God's glory is with us!

People: Praise God!

Offertory Invitation

The time of sacrifice is our time of sharing equally from what we have received. Mary and Joseph were poor. They only bought two pigeons when they presented the Lamb of God. Their offering demands our gifts of love.

Offertory Praise

Gracious and Generous Provider, your allowing Simeon and Anna to behold the Christ cheers our hearts. And we, too, have experienced the Messiah. Accept our meager tokens in humble gratitude. For we pray in the Messiah's matchless name.

Benediction

Leader: May the God of Strength bless you!

People: May the Spirit of wisdom bind us in unity.

Leader: May the Spirit of divine favor send you into all the world.

People: We will go, because God came to us!

Leader: Go in the peace and power of Christ!

People: We leave to be Christ, alive, in the world! Alleluia and amen!

WATCH NIGHT WORSHIP · DECEMBER 31

Ecclesiastes 3:1–13
Psalm 90
Matthew 25:31–46
Revelation 21:1–6

This is a service of African American congregations that began as people anticipated "watching out" the last year of slavery. The service of watching and waiting continues.

Watch night worship is a time for reflection, testimonies, and songs of God's grace. It is the period when we voice our determination for the gift of a year to come. Usually an intergenerational service, both youth and seasoned saints can play an important part. History meets the future. Tradition faces hopes. The God of the years is constant. Jesus is the same yesterday, today, and forever.

Altar Focus

A big clock with the hands stuck at five minutes to midnight sits on an altar covered with red, black, and green kente cloth. Implements of grinders, hoes, spades, and even an old cotton sack become the visual aids. A quilt draping the altar would be another useful article. Stalks of wheat, bolls of cotton, and even tobacco leaves can be placed in vases as "floral" arrangements.

Time is optional, of course. However, the ideal gathering is around a potluck dinner with games for all ages following. Worship should be begin around 10:30 P.M. Serving breakfast following worship allows the guns of salute to stop and the revelers to find their way inside!

Call to Worship

Leader: Why do we gather on this night?
People: We gather to remember our enslaved past.
Leader: Why do we gather on this night?
People: We gather to celebrate God's keeping powers.

Leader: Why do we gather on this night?
People: We gather to recall God's mercies in the midst of oppression.
Leader: Why do we gather this night?
People: We gather to celebrate our God who journeys with us, year by year.
All: Thanks be unto the ever faithful and true God.

Song of Praise

Call to Confession

The year is almost over. Many of the things we made covenant to do in January have fallen by the wayside. Let us seek forgiveness of our sin.

Silent Confession

Words of Assurance

Our sins are removed as far as the east is from the west. This is the promise of God. For our God yearns for authentic relationship with us. This is mighty good news.

Call to Remember

Remember God's goodness during the year. Many are the afflictions of the righteous, but God delivers us from them all. Those with willingness are provided these moments to testify to the ways God has sent victory our way.

Call to Prayer for the New Year

The year is almost over. Our elders taught us how to bow on our knees before the Almighty. Kneeling conveys our humble attitude before God. Kneeling is a symbol of our grateful hearts before the throne of Grace. Let us prepare now to kneel in prayer as we watch for the New Year. Let us praise God together on our knees.

A Covenant of Declarations

Happy New Year! Thank God for another opportunity to offer praise and thanksgiving to our Maker, Redeemer, and Sustainer. Resolutions often last until after breakfast! But our foreparents made their declarations of intentions for better Christian service as they were empowered by the Holy Spirit. As you are led, please rise and state your intentions to walk with Jesus in this New Year.

Offertory Invitation

Through the year God has been faithful. Our generous response through our sharing is how we say, "Thanks."

Offertory Praise

Beneficent and Gracious Savior, we cannot pay for one second of the year you have brought us through. Yet, we offer these tokens in humble appreciation that as others watch and wait in the coming years, these doors will be open to receive their grateful hearts. In the name of Love we pray.

Benediction

Leader: The old has passed and the New Year has arrived.
People: We have a new beginning.
Leader: The God of fresh starts has given us a brand new slate.
People: We leave to write new history with our Amazing God.
Leader: Go in the peace and power of the God who holds yesterday, today, and every tomorrow. Remember, you are blessed signs of God's renewing promises as you go your way rejoicing!
People: Amen.

HOLY NAME OF JESUS DAY · JANUARY 1

Numbers 6:22–27
Psalm 8
Galatians 4:4–7 or Philippians 2:5–13
Luke 2:15–21

Call to Worship

Leader: The Name Above All Names summons us today.
People: We have heard the calling of our names.
Leader: The Name Beyond Words commands an accounting.
People: We have heard the calling of our names.
Leader: The Name Above All Names has given us a new name.
People: We bless the wonderful name of Jesus!

Call to Confession

Too often we fail to live up to the name Christian. Confession restores the worth and value of our name. Let us offer our prayers of confession.

Confession

God, you have called us by name. Like children, at times we act as if we do not hear our names being called. Forgive us our sin. Restore us to full relationship with you. We long to walk worthy of your matchless name. It is in the name of Jesus that we pray.

Words of Assurance

We have been made in the image of God. We have been crowned with glory and honor. With our confession of sin we receive restoration of the right to bear the name. Glory to the majestic name of our Sovereign God.

Offertory Invitation

We are children of God, adopted into the royal family. We are heirs to salvation. It is our right to share in order that others may know about this wonderful relationship.

Offertory Praise

Lavishly Generous One, you have given us everything, including the right to wear the name of the Only Begotten Son. Accept these, our gifts, that others might come to wear and to bless his exalted name. In the name of Christ we pray. Amen.

Responsive Reading

Leader: God's name is a household word.
People: In all places across town the name of God is uplifted.
Leader: Babies and toddlers, primary youth, and rapping teens all call on the name of God.
People: Not all talk of God is holy!
Leader: Some God language is very profane.
People: Parents call upon the name of God.
Leader: Grandparents pray the name of God.
People: Sophisticated folks tip around this blessed name.
Leader: Idiots make every attempt to evade giving honor to the name of God.
People: Yet, without words, the name is spoken through the star spangled heavens.
Leader: Without articulation the name blazes in sunrises and sunsets.
People: The breeze through the trees echoes the name.
Leader: The tiny, fragile flower, pushing its way through concrete, shouts out the name.
People: Then, we look in the eyes of infants and those who are aging with grace and the matchless name is whispered again.
All: For God's name is a household word.

Benediction

Leader: The Lord bless you and keep you.
People: The Lord's face shine upon you.
Leader: The Lord be gracious unto you.
People: The countenance of the Lord be lifted upon you.
Leader: May the Lord, our God, grant you great shalom! Amen.
People: Hallelujah and amen.

THE SECOND SUNDAY AFTER CHRISTMAS

Jeremiah 31:7–14
Psalm 147:12–20
Ephesians 1:3–14
John 1:1–18

Call to Worship

Leader: Who wants to be a millionaire?
People: Excuse you! This is not some television show. We are in worship!
Leader: Who wants to be a millionaire?
People: We are already multimillionaires! God has more than blessed us in Christ with every spiritual blessing in the heavenly places. We have been adopted into the royal family. We are joint heirs with Christ. We simply gather to worship the Most High God, who is worthy of our praise.
All: Thanks be unto God, who has freely given us great grace in the Beloved.

Call to Confession

Jesus was in the world and the world did not know him. He came unto his own and they did not receive him. But all who receive him and believe in his name have power to be children of God. Confession makes us at one with God. Let us confess our sin.

Silent Confession

Words of Assurance

In Jesus Christ, we have obtained an inheritance, having been destined according to the purpose of him who accomplishes all things according to his counsel and will, so that we who have set our hope in Christ might live for the praise of his glory. By grace we are saved. This is good news!

Responsive Reading

Leader: God is worthy! God is worthy! God is worthy of our praise.
People: God's grace and strength have carried us through another week.

Leader: Our children have been blessed. God's mercy keeps them covered.
People: God's Word is alive in our midst. We stand on the promises and refuse to simply exist on the premises.
Leader: The seasons are faithful, reminding us of God's steadfast love.
People: Who can stand before the awesome God?
Leader: The elements sing of God's glory. Every season has its song of praise.
People: God's Word is faithful and true. The promise is that the last shall be first.
All: It is our time! Worthy is our God!

Offertory Invitation

In the beginning was the Word, and the Word was with God, and the Word was God. With grateful hearts let us share, that the Word may continue to be spread.

Offertory Praise

True Light, who enlightens everyone, we appreciate your coming into the world. Receive these our meager gifts. In the name of the Light of the World we pray.

Benediction

Leader: The Word has become flesh and has come to live among us.
People: We are the light of the world.
Leader: The world needs to see and to know the Light.
People: We are the light of the world.
Leader: The Word is flesh and lives in you.
People: We are the light of the world! It is so, now and forever more.

4 · THE SEASON OF EPIPHANY

The Greco-Roman world gave us the word *epiphany*. Epiphany designated for them the occasion when state officials made public appearances within the provinces. The early Church adopted the term to indicate the manifestations of Christ within the world. During Epiphany we get different snapshots of the Savior's brilliant glory.

The Greek word *epiphaneia* means to manifest, show forth, or make clear. The bright star of Bethlehem guided the Wise to get a glimpse of the newborn Sovereign. During this season of illumination, many sightings of the Divine will help us view the many-faceted aspects of our great Savior and the plan for our salvation.

January 6 is the official Feast of Epiphany. This date signals the arrival of the known world to give honor and treasure to Jesus and also signifies his baptism by John when the full Trinity is displayed.

The intent of the month of January in general is new beginnings, fresh starts, and the additional opportunities God supplies for us. Its theme can be the light of justice. Epiphany, baptismal renewal, and the Dr. Martin Luther King, Jr. celebration are priorities of this month.

Altar Focus

To symbolize light, a large, old-fashioned kerosene lamp can be the altar focus for the first Sunday in January. A menorah, with black, red, and green candles, can be placed between the usual Christ candles. When Epiphany is celebrated on the Sunday nearest January 6, the altar focus can feature water pitchers of various shapes and sizes, goblets, crystal decanters, and treasure chests. This is another liturgical day of white, and gold stars will enhance the world's "illumination."

On the Sunday that reaffirmation of baptism is celebrated, a large, clear, crystal bowl filled with water or one of the "heritage" wash basins and pitchers can be featured. Conch shells, dried sponges, and assorted sea shells call out, "Take me to the water!"[11] The baptismal font and other symbols of baptism are welcomed. The Sunday nearest January 6 is the opportune day for celebrating baptismal renewal.

For Dr. King's celebration, a grapevine wreath may be the altar focus, wrapped in black, red, and green cloth or paper, with large red flowers having yellow centers, to represent our homeland and our continuing struggle for liberty and justice. The altar need not be fully changed weekly, but enhanced for the particular liturgical setting of worship.

EPIPHANY

Isaiah 60:1–6
Psalm 72:1–14
Ephesians 3:1–12
Matthew 2:1–12

Call to Worship

Leader: Have you not heard? Did you not know? Christ went to Africa!
People: What in the world do you mean?
Leader: God sent the Light of the World to Africa!
People: Why did this happen?
Leader: The spirit of death was seeking to extinguish the Light. Africa was hospitable and welcomed her son home.
People: Let's give the Radiant God praise for a goodly land that provided refuge for the Hope of the World!

Responsive Reading

Leader: Warrior God, we praise you for the reign of your son.
People: He came to judge the poor with justice and your inheritance with righteousness.
Leader: We continue to pray that Jesus Christ will defeat our foes, root out systems of poverty, and send us deliverance from every oppressor.
People: Jesus, our elder brother, has lived among us since the generations of the ancestors.
Leader: May his loving ways be like fresh rain, which showers the earth and her inhabitants.
People: Our hearts long for his reign of right living and abiding peace.
Leader: May the world's leaders render their hearts to his leading. May the rulers of every province and tribe bring the sacrifice of their willing spirit. May the wealthy and the greedy bow before him in reverence and in honor.
People: For their hearts are yet in God's hands. And without God we have no help.
Leader: But we have received mercy from God in our past.

People: From oppression and violence, God has redeemed our life. Those who have died, struggling for justice, are precious in the sight of our God. *Unison:* God preserves the lives of those who are in need!

Call to Confession

The Light has come and too often we refuse to acknowledge its presence. Let us confess our preference for the absence of illumination.

Confession

Lord of light and ability to see, we confess our sin of ignoring you and refusing to open our eyes to your radiance. Your light causes us to look inward to change, and not outward to blame others. Your light pulls us up to action instead of down in hopelessness. Your light means transformation and change. Your light scares us! Forgive us, we pray, for our sin.

Words of Assurance

Lift up your eyes and look around; the glory of the Lord shines on you and in you! Your sons and your daughters shall see and be radiant! Your heart shall thrill and rejoice, because abundance and the wealth of nations shall come to you. Praise the Lord!

Offertory Invitation

The wise of every generation know to open their treasures to the Inspiration of Glory. The Wise offered what they had. This privilege is ours today.

Offertory Praise

Jesus Christ came and opened his treasure chest of inheritance unto us. Now we have access to God and boldness and confidence through faith in him. So that the world might know this birthright, we offer what is ours. In the name of the Giver, we pray.

Benediction

Leader: The star is yet shining and people are yet looking for the Light of the World!
People: We leave to point the way.
Leader: The manger is empty, and the angelic choir no longer sings.
People: Christ is at home in our hearts! His song of victory is on our lips.
Leader: The light of Christ will lead you, the love of Christ will enfold you, and the spirit of Christ will live through you, world without end! Amen and amen!

THE FIRST SUNDAY AFTER EPIPHANY · BAPTISM OF THE LORD

Genesis 1:1–15
Psalm 29
Acts 19:1–7
Mark 1:4–11

Call to Worship

Leader: This is a day to recall God's love affair with water!
People: This is a day to remember our baptisms with thankfulness.
Leader: This is a day to recall the embryonic fluids of our birth.
People: This same water delivered God's chosen people through the Exodus!
Leader: This is the very water that delivered us from our sin into salvation.
People: This is a day of great thanksgiving to the God who loves water!

Call to Confession

In the beginning God called, and chaos gave way to order and beauty. This is our call for the sinful chaos in our life to give way with our confession. Let us turn to God.

Confession

Great God, we have heard your call to move from the disorder of our lives. We have gathered because we cannot do it alone. We come to ask your forgiveness of our sin. Wash us clean. Remove our bent toward sin and sinfulness. Give us willing hearts to follow you, your Word, and your divine way. Mark us afresh this day with the washing of your Holy Spirit, we pray in the matchless name of the Christ Child who was born to die in our place. May it be so now and always.

Words of Assurance

The voice of God thunders over the waters. And the voice of God speaks forgiveness to our parched and weary spirits. The cleansing power of God has restored us to right relationship. This is mighty good news.

Responsive Reading

Leader: God, we join with the angels and call out a shout of "Bravo!"
People: We have come to offer our meager worship to you who are robed in holy splendor.
Leader: We have come dressed in our best and realize that our inner lives are as filthy rags before your holiness.
People: As we enter this sacred place, your holiness overwhelms us and we see our need for cleansing.
Leader: In this sanctuary the voice of God thunders!
People: The brilliant holiness of God thunders throughout the earth.
Leader: We stand in awe before the magnificent greatness of God.
People: The symphonic thunders of God call out reminders of God's majesty.
Leader: It is God who thunders over the waters.
People: God's thunder smashes, skips, topples, jumps, and sets trees to dancing.
Leader: God's thunder invites, enfolds, baptizes, dips, sprinkles, gushes, and enmeshes us into the mystery of our faith.
People: God is enthroned above the waters—powerful, majestic, and providing us with strength.
All: The God of thundering and of still waters gives all the people great shalom!

Offertory Invitation

John baptized with the waters of repentance, telling people to believe in Jesus Christ who was to come. Jesus has come. We have found deliverance from our sin. Our giving makes room for others to come and to believe. Let's share in this hope.

Offertory Praise

People across the world have the invitation to come and be baptized in the name of Jesus Christ. With our offerings we give thanks for the privilege of spreading this good news. In the name of the Beloved, we pray.

Benediction

Leader: Leave! Remember that your baptism has named you Beloved.
People: We go to take our new name in action throughout the world we touch.

Leader: Leave! Remember that your baptism has claimed you as an heir of God!

People: We go to live as those who have the inheritance of Love within their hearts.

Leader: Leave! Remember that your baptism has given you access to the keeping power of the Holy Spirit! Walk in creative power. Act with holy boldness. Touch gently with the amazing grace of one baptized into the Royal Family.

People: We go to represent the Holy Trinity in all the world! Hallelujah and amen.

THE SECOND SUNDAY AFTER EPIPHANY
1 Samuel 3:1–10 (11–20)
Psalm 139:1–18
1 Corinthians 6:12–20
John 1:43–51

Call to Worship
Leader: The search continues. The call is out. God is looking for those who will represent God.
People: Here I am, Lord. Send me.
Leader: There are people crying. There are people dying. There are people who need hope.
People: Here I am, Lord. Send me.
Leader: There is much depression, much despair, much pain.
People: Here I am, Lord. Send me.
Leader: In this season of Epiphany, God is searching for those who will twinkle in their places.
People: Lord, we have heard your call. We are here. Speak. Your servants are listening.

Call to Confession
The noise of this world makes us deaf to the small, still, and quiet voice of the Holy One. In these sacred moments we can confess our sin and listen for God as the inner clamor ceases. Let us center down.

Silent Confession

Confession
God, we confess that too often we do not hear you call. The real deal is that we get so busy doing our own thing until we forget to listen! Yet, we long to hear a fresh word from you. Forgive us our sin. Speak to our hearts. We are listening. We will obey. In the name of Jesus Christ, we pray.

Words of Assurance
Hear the good news. Confession clears our hearts and opens our ears. God has already spoken words of forgiveness and amazing grace. Let your hearts be glad!

Responsive Reading

Leader: God the investigator has been on the case!

People: God knows all the facts of our lives. They are not all good!

Leader: Our lives are like open books to God.

People: Before we speak, the thoughts we think are revealed unto God.

Leader: We cannot escape the clutches of the Almighty.

People: We are never out of God's sight.

Leader: When we leave, when we get back, is insignificant—for God already has the news.

People: It's overwhelming to realize that there is no spot that God is not!

Leader: It's mind boggling to recognize that God encompasses all we say, think, or do.

People: It's reassuring to come to grips with this reality—God is always near.

Leader: God knew us before we were formed in our mother's womb.

People: We are wonderful! We are awesome! We are made in the image of the divine.

Leader: You can't stop being wonderful! The Wonder-Working God has decreed that you're wonderful! Live like it!

People: We worship and praise the Awesome Maker of us all! The case is closed. We're wonderful!

Offertory Invitation

God's thoughts toward us are more than the numbers of sand. We cannot count the many and various ways that God works on our behalf. Let us show our inadequate appreciation by sharing with others.

Offertory Praise

High God, receive these our tokens of gratitude in thanks for all you do for us. May these offerings be used to spread your name, your power, and your glory throughout the earth. We pray in the name of your son, Jesus Christ.

Benediction

Leader: Leave to be the Church everywhere you go!

People: We leave remembering that all things are lawful but not beneficial.

Leader: Leave to let the world see Jesus shining through your life!

People: We leave knowing that we have been called to bring others.

Leader: Leave remembering that you are wonderful!

People: We leave in the knowledge of whose we are—wonderful offspring of a wonder-working God! This is truly our good news! Amen.

THE THIRD SUNDAY AFTER EPIPHANY

Jonah 3:1–5, 10
Psalm 62:5–12
1 Corinthians 7:29–31
Mark 1:14–20

Call to Worship

Leader: Jonah, God is calling you to accountability!
People: We have come to worship. There is no Jonah in our midst!
Leader: Jonah, God is calling you to accountability!
People: We have gathered in this place with those like us to offer God thanks and praise.
Leader: Jonah, God is calling you to accountability!
People: We don't want to hear about "those people, out there." This is our time. This is our sacred space. For today, we need encouragement for ourselves.
Leader: Jonah, God is calling you to accountability! "Those people" are your assignment!
People: Lord, the Jonah in us wants to run. But we have come to offer you praise. Feed us in this hour so that we might feed others when we leave.

Call to Confession

God sent Jonah to tell people he did not like about a message of God's grace. Jonah was reluctant to give the Ninevites the message because they were Israel's worst enemy. Yet God was willing to forgive them if they confessed and repented. Today this is our opportunity to confess our sin and receive deliverance from God's wrath. Let us pray.

Confession

God, we don't want to go to those who have oppressed us with a message of your forgiveness. Why, we really don't want to ask for forgiveness for our own sin, because it makes us feel bad. However, our sin is plainly before us. Forgive us, we pray. Restore us to your divine favor in order that we might go and spread your love.

Words of Assurance

When God saw that the people of Nineveh turned from their wicked ways, the calamity was turned away. With the confession of our sin we, too, are delivered from the judgment of a righteous God. This is good news. Thanks be unto God.

Responsive Reading

Leader: The One and Only God awaits the return of our souls in silence.
People: All that we need, God has to supply.
Leader: God is solid as a rock. God is the source of our salvation. God is our mighty fortress.
People: We can rest our case on the honor of God's reputation alone.
Leader: Our trust is in this God who is a fortified place of refuge.
People: Those who trust in their status and position are just one breath away from death.
Leader: Those born to stations of lowliness can receive granite strength from the Absolute God!
People: Our help and safe harbor is in God. We lay our lives on the line with the Ancient of Days.

Offertory Invitation

We can put no confidence in extortion nor will we set our vain hopes on the gains from robbery. Riches cannot save us. Our only help comes from the Lavishly Generous God. Let's trust in this God as we share our tithes and offerings.

Offertory Praise

Steadfast love belongs to you, O God. It is you who will repay us all according to our work for you, our faith in you and our returning a just portion unto you. Accept our offerings in the name of your son, Jesus Christ.

Benediction

Leader: My sisters and my brothers, the present form of this world is passing away.
People: The appointed time for completing our assignments is growing short.
Leader: Wear this world as a loose garment. God is sending you to Nineveh.
People: We are Jonah. We have received our assignments to tell the message to all, even those we don't like!
Leader: Go! Tell the message with love. Deliver the message with grace. And be the message with power! The God who called you to send you has gone before you! Walk in confidence. Live on purpose! Shine for God everywhere you go!

THE FOURTH SUNDAY AFTER EPIPHANY

Deuteronomy 18:15–20
Psalm 111
1 Corinthians 8:1–13
Mark 1:21–28

Call to Worship

Leader: God is here!
People: When God shows up, we are on the alert.
Leader: God is among us!
People: We long to see God in the sanctuary.
Leader: God is within you and me.
People: It's our time to make God look good in all the earth. We antici-
pate good news to help us make God look good. We come to worship.

Call to Confession

The people of God have always made plenty of promises. They promised
that if God raised up a prophet from among them they would listen. We
find it so difficult to listen to anything but what we want to hear. It's time
to confess our sin.

Confession

God, you call us to be accountable. Your Word declares that if we do not
live up to the words of life that we would surely die. We have sinned. We
have not done your will in the way you have decreed. Forgive our sin.
Restore us to communion with you and the congregation of the righteous. We pray in the matchless name of the Light of the World.

Words of Assurance

The reverence of God is the beginning of wisdom. Those who practice
confession show good understanding. Our confession is to the praise of
God. We are forgiven. This is good news.

Responsive Reading

Leader: All that is within me shouts out praise unto Worthy God.
People: God's benefits and loving kindness cause me to give thanks with
my whole being.

Leader: It's testimony time, for God certainly has been good.
People: God's worthy works deserve telling, for they are endless.
Leader: God's generosity never runs out and the miracles keep on coming our way!
People: God's Word is sure. We've checked the record, studied the accounts, and God's record is one of excellence and endurance.
Leader: God has a proven record in the earth. God is faithful and just.
People: God has no short supply and the covenant endures forever.
Leader: The power of God's own hand is legend. God's Word cannot fail.
People: We serve and worship the Awesome God, whose praise is forevermore.

Offertory Invitation

Anyone who loves God is known and claimed by God. Anyone who loves God also loves the people of God and loves those who have not come to know God in the pardon of their sin. Our sharing our temporal means allows the Love of God to continue to be spread in all the world. Let's share out of our love for God.

Offertory

The promise is that when we give it shall be given back to us, pressed down, shaken together, and running over. We look for the increase as we have shared in the giving. We offer these gifts in the name of Love.

Benediction

Leader: When Jesus taught, the people were astonished at his teaching. For he taught as one with authority. That authority is now in our hands. Go, teaching the Word.
People: We leave to teach what we have learned. We are the lights of the world.
Leader: Jesus cast out demons and healed the sick. That same power is now in our hands. Go, being healing agents in the world.
People: We leave to pass along the healing we have received. We are the lights of the world.
Leader: Go! The Authority, the Healer, and the Power go with you and before you!
People: Hallelujah and amen!

THE FIFTH SUNDAY AFTER EPIPHANY

Isaiah 40:21–31
Psalm 147:1–11, 20
1 Corinthians 9:16–23
Mark 1:29–39

Call to Worship

Leader: Have you not known? Have you not heard? Our God is the ever-lasting God, the Creator of the ends of the earth.
People: Our God does not grow faint or weary and has understanding that is unknowable.
Leader: Our God gives power to the faint and strength to the powerless.
People: Even the young will faint and grow weary, falling exhausted by the way.
Leader: But there is a promise to those who will wait on God.
People: Our strength shall be renewed. We shall mount with the wings of eagles. We shall run and not be weary. We shall walk and not faint.
Teach us, dear God, how to wait!

Call to Confession

The word "wait" is not one that we like to consider. We want "instant." And too often when God calls us to "wait" we run ahead, get into trouble, and sin. This is our time to confess. Let us pray.

Confession

God, we proclaim the gospel and yet it gives us no ground for boasting. For this places an obligation upon us to live the gospel that we preach. We have sinned and fallen short of your Word. Forgive us we pray, in Jesus' name.

Words of Assurance

God takes good pleasure in those who confess and repent from their hearts. Our hope in the faithfulness of God's restoring power is that we are granted absolution and restoration. This is good news.

Responsive Reading

Leader: Sing a song of wild delight to the God who is gracious and generous.

People: God has restored our lives, rebuilt our lives, and lifted us from the pits of oppression.

Leader: The healing God has provided a soothing balm for our many wounds.

People: This God knows us intimately, for the Creator has given names to the gazillion of stars.

Leader: Great is God and abundant in power. We cannot measure the goodness of God.

People: Limitless strength and unfailing mercy are provided for the outcast and the neglected.

Leader: Hymns of glad songs burst forth from our lips.

People: We sing with the whole earth new songs of unending praise. We will keep melodies of thanksgiving within our heart.

Leader: God is not impressed by strength or knowledge.

People: Those who honor God will receive both attention and strength to press on.

All: Peace will be at our borders, our children will be blessed, and our communities will be secure. It's time to rehearse our new songs unto God!

Offertory Invitation

Because God is great in strength and mighty in power, no one who calls in faith will be turned away. God is calling us by name. Let us share our resources to ensure that the call is heard around the world.

Offertory Praise

God, you have given us such a great reward, the gift of salvation. You gave it to us free of charge. We offer our gifts for the sake of the gospel that all may share in its blessings. Receive them in the name of Jesus Christ.

Benediction

Leader: People are yet searching for signs of the Christ.

People: We return to our neighborhoods, our schools, our jobs, and our homes to share the good news. We want the world to see Jesus in our lives!

Leader: Jesus didn't travel far, but the message of salvation spread.

People: Wherever we go, the good news will be shared!

Leader: Go! The commission to make new disciples is ours. And the power belongs to us!

THE SIXTH SUNDAY AFTER EPIPHANY

2 Kings 5:1–14
Psalm 30
1 Corinthians 9:24–27
Mark 1:40–45

Call to Worship

Leader: We are called to a time of forgetting!
People: We are called to worship. We come to offer God praise.
Leader: We are called to a time of forgetting that which is past and done.
People: God is doing a new thing in the earth. Our worry about the old retards our worship.
Leader: We are called to a time of forgetting as the new springs forth. Oh, say, can you see it?
People: We are witnesses that God is a way maker. Our God gives water in wilderness places and makes rivers to flow in deserts. Our God is an awesome God. And we await the new!

Call to Confession

God has called us "chosen." God has formed us for praise and worship. Yet, we have bogged ourselves down in worry and doubt. We have dishonored God with our sin. It's time for confession.

Confession

God, we have not honored you but burdened and wearied you with our sin. Forgive us our sin and cleanse us from our iniquities, we pray in the name of the Soon-Coming Sovereign.

Words of Confession

God has promised that through our confession our sin is blotted out and remembered no more. This is good news! Thanks be to the God of every new beginning.

Responsive Reading

Leader: What a mighty God we serve, who gives dignity to those who are down and out.

People: It is right and good to celebrate the amazing God who protects us and delivers us from trouble.

Leader: We are safe in the arms of the Almighty, who does not allow our enemies to have victory over us.

People: Even in our times of illness, God is like a faithful nurse, always attending our needs and bringing us back to health.

Leader: It is marvelous to be able to pray, "God, be gracious unto me, raise me up" and to know the Almighty hears.

People: While my enemies wait for my death, making bets on my certain defeat, it is God who lifts me up.

Leader: When the very one I thought was a friend turned on me, God has never failed to be a constant friend.

People: The amazing grace of God has established me again and again. Every time I shout out the victory.

Leader: Your enemy will never prevail against the God who is pleased with your life and honors your integrity.

People: We are forever in the presence of the all-seeing God. From everlasting to everlasting, God is the same. Faithful. True. Steadfast. The Ultimate Amen.

Offertory Invitation

Every promise of God is "Yes!" and "Amen!" For this reason we can offer our tokens in gratitude.

Offertory Praise

God, we thank you for establishing us in Christ and anointing us with the gift of the Holy Spirit. Use these, our gifts, to bring others into your fold, we pray in the name of the Great Amen.

Benediction

Leader: Healing has been provided. Take up your mats and go! Be an epiphany of the Christ!

People: Healing has been received. We leave to spread this good news wherever we go.

Leader: God has forgiven our sin. Go in that authority to live lives of victory and triumph!

People: Salvation enfolds us. Our sin is covered. We go to be images of Christ in the world.

Leader: Go in the Name of the Creator, with the victory of the Healer and the power of the Keeper!

People: Hallelujah and amen!

THE SEVENTH SUNDAY AFTER EPIPHANY

Isaiah 43:18–25
Psalm 41
2 Corinthians 1:18–22
Mark 2:1–12

Call to Worship

Leader: The God of the new calls us to gather.
People: We come longing to put old ways behind us.
Leader: Yesterday is gone. Tomorrow is not promised.
People: Today is our fresh start and our new beginning.
Leader: Do not remember the former things or consider the things of old.
People: God is about to do a new thing; now it springs forth. God makes ways in the wilderness and rivers in the desert. For all things new, we come to offer our praise.

Call to Confession

God's grace and mercy are fresh and new. But our sinful ways are constant. God is burdened with our sins and weary with our iniquities. This is our time to confess and to repent so that our transgressions will be remembered no more. Let us pray.

Confession

God of yesterday, today, and tomorrow, we approach you with reverence and awe. On this, another new day, we give you honor for this chance to approach your throne of grace. Our old behaviors sicken us and bring grief to your heart. Forgive us. Renew us. Restore us to right relationship with you, we pray in the name of Jesus, the Christ.

Words of Assurance

It is God who establishes us in Christ and has anointed us by giving us the seal of the Holy Spirit in our hearts. This is good news. We are made brand new. Thanks be unto God.

Responsive Reading

Leader: God is watching and on alert for those who will offer care and concern for the poor.

People: God's delight is in those with honest concern for the "little people."
Leader: Those who go out of their way to be in ministry with the last, the least, and the neglected are protected by the Almighty.
People: The healing hand of God is extended toward those who reach out to uplift all who are oppressed.
Leader: Many are they who wish we were wiped out of existence.
People: They utter meaningless words, enact inadequate legislation, and plot ways to eradicate civil rights, equal opportunity, and fair housing laws.
Leader: Mischief is their constant thought.
People: Evil lies within their hearts as they scheme for our destruction.
Leader: They have wished for every deadly disease to destroy us.
People: They have spread the worst lies about us.
Leader: They have even turned us against each other.
People: But the graciousness of God has prevailed and we are yet alive.
Leader: Because we remember the poor, care for the ill, feed the hungry, clothe the naked, and tend to the imprisoned, our enemies have not won!
People: Our integrity caused God to smile upon us.
Leader: We are sustained by God's presence.
People: We bless the God of yesterday, today, and forever. From everlasting to everlasting, God is always the same!

Call to Offering

In God every promise is "Yes!" And God is faithful in keeping every promise. Therefore, we can give liberally, knowing that God will more than repay our gifts. Let us share from our abundance.

Offertory Praise

God, we give to your glory. We thank you for this chance to take part in helping to spread your realm throughout the world. Receive our tangible love in the name of Jesus Christ, we pray.

Benediction

Leader: Our time of community refreshing is over!
People: It is time for us individually to go to work.
Leader: Our time of sitting and receiving is over!
People: It is time for us to take Jesus into the streets.
Leader: Our time of being in church is finished!
People: It's time for us to go into the world and be the Church!
Leader: Stand up. Pick up your things. Walk into the world, with boldness. Go, with the Love, the Redemption, and the Power of the Trinity!
People: Hallelujah and amen!

THE EIGHTH SUNDAY AFTER EPIPHANY

Hosea 2:14–20
Psalm 103:1–13, 22
2 Corinthians 3:1–6
Mark 2:13–22

Call to Worship

Leader: This is a day of great love when God calls the whoring bride to come home!
People: You sound like a rap artist talking about whores in worship!
Leader: The Church is the Bride of Christ. She has always gone in search of other lovers.
People: We don't talk about that on Sunday mornings. This is God's day.
Leader: And it is God who is calling the backslidden heifer to come home!
People: What will God do to one who has done wrong and committed sin?
Leader: God has promised that when she returns she will be a wife beloved forever.
People: It's time to return home to the God of righteousness, justice, mercy, and steadfast love. This day we offer God earnest and sincere praise!

Call to Confession

God wants to renew the marriage covenant with the Bride of Christ. Sin is in the way. We have this time to confess our sin. Shall we pray?

Confession

God, we have allowed ourselves to be drawn away by the lying words of other lovers who have failed to provide us with security. We repent of our sin. We seek your forgiveness. We want to come home to you. Renew the covenant, we pray, in the name of the Bridegroom.

Words of Assurance

With our confession, the promise from God is that "I will take you for my wife in faithfulness; and you shall know the Lord." This is good news.

Responsive Reading

Leader: It's time to raise the roof in praise to the Sovereign God.

People: From the rising of the sun to the going down of the same, God is worthy to be praised.

Leader: Let our soul recount the many blessings we have received from God's hands. Name them one by one.

People: There is not adequate time allotted to list all the blessings we have been given.

Leader: God forgives all our sin. God heals all our diseases. God redeemed our life from hell.

People: God has crowned us with loving kindness, tender mercy, and steadfast love.

Leader: God has wrapped us in eternal goodness and satisfied us with good so that our youth is renewed.

People: God is on the side of the oppressed, merciful, slow to anger, and gracious in mercy.

Leader: God does not treat us with contempt. God has never kicked us aside. God does not keep fussing, cussing, or arguing with us, even when we have turned our backs and turned away!

People: God never pays us back tit for tat! As far as the heavens are above the earth, so great is the amazing love of God towards those who walk in pure love. As far as the east is from the west, as far as sunrise is from sunset is how far God removes our sin when we confess. Great is the compassion of our God. Everything within me lifts in praise to the mention of God's name.

Offertory Invitation

We don't need personal letters of recommendation to speak to us about the faithfulness of God toward us. It's our time to prove our faithfulness in return for all we have already received. Let's give with grateful hearts.

Offertory Praise

God, we surely are not competent of ourselves to claim any good within ourselves. We recognize that our competence comes from you who have made us competent to be ministers of the New Covenant written in the blood of your only Begotten Son. We thank you for the gifts of the Holy Spirit at work in us, moving us to share what we have received. Use them to further the work of your realm. We offer them in the name of the Risen Christ.

Benediction

Leader: "Follow me," Jesus called, wanting others to become reflections of him.

People: We leave to follow in the footsteps of Christ and show the world what God looks like with flesh on!

Leader: "Follow me," Jesus called as he ate with sinners and visited with those who were suspect.

People: We leave to follow Jesus, doing what he would do, offering grace to all.

Leader: "Follow me," Jesus called as he prepared others to be ready when he comes again.

People: We leave to follow Jesus, allowing new wine to be put in fresh wineskins.

Leader: The creative abilities of God, the ministering spirit of Christ, and the holy boldness of the Holy Spirit go with us as we follow Jesus.

People: Hallelujah and amen.

THE NINTH SUNDAY AFTER EPIPHANY

Deuteronomy 5:12–15
Psalm 81:1–10
2 Corinthians 4:5–12
Mark 2:23–3:6

Call to Worship

Leader: Observe the Sabbath day and keep it holy as God commands.
People: Six days we have labored, but this day is holy unto God.
Leader: This is a day of Sabbath rest.
People: We were slaves and God delivered us with a mighty outstretched hand. This is a day for giving thanks unto the Delivering God.

Call to Confession

The commandments have been broken. We have defiled the laws of God. It is time for confession of the sin within us. Let us pray.

Confession

God, we would like to forget your laws and do things our own way. And through the week we pretend that we are god. Yet, our lives are out of order. We come to ask you to forgive our sin and restore us to right relationship. We recognize that you are Sovereign indeed.

Words of Assurance

God is faithful and just to forgive us our sin and cleanse us from all unrighteousness. This is our salvation. Thanks be unto God.

Responsive Reading

Leader: Let's call out a strong shout to the Almighty, who is strength beyond measure.
People: We will raise the roof with our singing, whip the tambourines, jazz up the guitars, pump up the horns, and make this a mighty day of celebration for the Holy One.

Leader: The choir will harmonize in anthems. The elders will moan out a metered hymn. And the youth will make a rap appropriate to speak their praise unto the Voice Beyond Voices.

People: This day is a reminder of how far God has brought us.

Leader: Never can we forget the benefits of El Shadai, our provider.

People: We have been freed from the shackles of slavery. The rod of oppression has been removed.

Leader: Straight up, we owe Jehovah big time praise and worship.

People: We will serve no other gods. The High God's praise fills our mouth forever more.

Offertory Invitation

God has shone in our hearts to give us the light of the knowledge of God's glory in the very face of Jesus Christ. Now, we have this treasure in earthen vessels. As we share our resources with others, it becomes clear that the power belongs to God.

Offertory Praise

Gracious God, we acknowledge that Jesus Christ is Lord of the Sabbath. And we offer these gifts in honor of his blessed name. May they be used to spread his work in the world, we pray.

Benediction

Leader: We leave, knowing that we will be afflicted in every way this week.

People: But we will not be crushed.

Leader: We leave, knowing that we will be perplexed this week.

People: But we will not be driven to despair.

Leader: We leave, knowing that we will be struck down this week.

People: But we will not be destroyed.

Leader: We carry within us the death and resurrection of Jesus Christ.

People: We are an Easter people and rising is our constant theme of praise.

Leader: Go in the power of God's ability to raise you in every situation. Let Christ be visible in all you say and do as you go, in the name of the Risen Christ.

People: Hallelujah and amen.

THE LAST SUNDAY AFTER EPIPHANY
TRANSFIGURATION SUNDAY

2 Kings 2:1–12
Psalm 50:1–6
2 Corinthians 4:3–6
Mark 9:2–9

Call to Worship

Leader: The Court is called to order!
People: The Righteous Judge is in the house!
Leader: The Court is called to order!
People: The docket is set for praise.
Leader: The Court is called to order!
People: We are attentive to the worship of this hour for our God lives and is present even now!

Call to Confession

Elisha asked for a double portion of Elijah's spirit before he ascended in a whirlwind into heaven. The double portion was promised if he could see the man of God being lifted up. God longs to give us a double portion! But our hearts have to be made ready to see the Living God. This calls for our confession. Let us pray.

Confession

God, we have been blinded by the little gods of this present world and have allowed our eyes to be taken from you. Forgive us our sin. Pour out that promised double portion of your Holy Spirit upon us that we might keep covenant with you. We pray in the name of Jesus, the Christ.

Words of Assurance

It is the good will of God who has shone in our hearts to give to us the light of the knowledge of the glory of God in the face of Jesus Christ. This is good news!

Responsive Reading

Leader: Here comes the Judge! Here comes the Judge! Get ready, friends, for here comes the Judge!

People: Out of Zion, the symbol of earthly beauty, the Righteous Judge calls us to assemble.

Leader: God arrives with great noise and fury. The Judge demands the appearance of all those who have sworn to a covenant relationship. Great fireworks of brilliance, a consuming fire, comes before the Judge.

People: The Judge summons us. The cosmos swears to the faithfulness of God. What about us? How do we answer in the days of the appearance of the Judge?

Leader: Here comes the Judge! Here comes the Judge! Get ready, friends, for here comes the Judge!

Offertory Invitation

We have seen the transforming light of the gospel of the glory of Christ, who is the very image of God. With our giving we do not proclaim ourselves; we proclaim Jesus Christ as Risen Lord and ourselves as slaves for the sake of helping to spread this good news. It's our time to give thanks to the God who blesses us with double portions!

Offertory Praise

El Shaddai, God of more than enough, we bless you for the ability to share. For you supply all our needs and there is no area of lack in our lives. You give us more than a double portion so that we abound in all things. Thank you for blessing us with the exceeding, abundant, and above all we can think, ask, or imagine. Receive these our tangible acts of praise.

Benediction

Leader: Beloved, leave this place of sanctuary and be love in the world.

People: We are beloved and named by God.

Leader: Beloved, leave this time of worship and be a blessing in the workplace.

People: We are beloved and claimed by God.

Leader: Beloved, leave this joyful music and be the melody this world needs to hear.

People: We are beloved and will sing in harmony with all we meet.

Leader: Beloved, leave this place of transfiguration and walk the face of the earth with peace.

People: We leave to be love and agents of transformation in all the places and with all the people we will touch.

Leader: Be love with the Maker of Music, the Harmony of Heaven, and the Melody Maker as your constant hymn of praise.

All: Hallelujah and amen.

5 · THE SEASON OF LENT

We become pilgrims on the forty-day journey, seeking our way out of the wilderness of sin in the season of Lent. It is a serious period of spiritual discipline as we either give up something pleasant or take on a new mission to enable others. Lent is our individual struggle to subdue our flesh and to wrestle with the sin issue, which tempts us so readily.

The early church prepared new members, catechumens, for Easter Sunday baptism. There was an intense year of being indoctrinated into the faith community. Both instructors and students of the faith fasted, prayed, studied, and made themselves more consciously aware of the sacrifice of Jesus Christ.

The Israelites wandered forty years in the wilderness. Jesus spent forty days and nights struggling with Satan in the wilderness. We will journey through our own forty-day wilderness, knowing that resurrection is on the way.

It is good to note that Sundays are not included in the forty-day Lenten period. For each Sunday worship experience is a reenactment of the resurrection!

Altar Focus

As the drama of Lent unfolds, with its journey toward the cross and resurrection, the altar should set the tempo for meditation and reflection. A Lenten garden might be a possibility for you. Local florists will gather the necessary plants and rent them for the season. Included should be any plant that will remind us of the Garden of Gethsemane, the place where Jesus spent his hours anticipating death for us.

Stalks of wheat and vines should be heavily emphasized as Jesus is the Bread of Life and the Vine from which we are nourished. Wheat was most likely the most important crop in that period. A huge rock or simulated boulder should be included to remind us of wise and foolish persons who select to build their faith on rock or sand. Perhaps a quiet waterfall might be included so that your altar would attract members during the weeks ahead, as a sacred spot for stopping to take a drink from the Fountain of Life, which never runs dry. Let your imagination flow and allow the artistry of your worship committee to make the garden one to remember. If you place lilies around the altar the day before Easter, the beauty will be striking!

This period of the church's year also includes Women's History Month in March. International Women's History Day is March 8. A "Worship for International Women's History Observance" is included on page 199 in chapter 8, "Additional Services."

ASH WEDNESDAY

Joel 2:1–2, 12–17
Psalm 51:1–17
2 Corinthians 5:20–6:10
Matthew 6:1–6, 16–21

Call to Worship

Read the Joel passage.

Have children dressed as clowns come in with garden implements and dirty hands. They are silent as they walk from the ear and nod, smiling at each row. They notice the cross at the altar and make attempts to kneel. But their dirty hands prevent them. One of the adult leaders, dressed as a clown, comes and offers to each child a sanitary handiwipe. They cleanse their hands and go kneel, signifying clean hearts before God. The children offer each of the congregation a handiwipe. Then a time of silent prayer is offered.

Call to Confession

Use the Psalm passage as responsive confession. Allow time for silent confession.

Words of Assurance

For our sake God made Jesus, who knew no sin, to be sin so that in him we might become the righteousness of God. See, now is the acceptable time, with our confession; now is the day of salvation. This is mighty good news.

Reading of the Gospel

Imposition of Ashes

(The palm branches of the preceding Palm Sunday are burned to become the necessary ashes. If they are not handy, a local florist or Catholic bookstore will have them available for purchase. Ash Wednesday is an occasion to remember our mortality and help us prepare for the six-week journey to the Resurrection Event, which is to come and mark us with eternal life!)

Offertory Invitation

We will not put any obstacle in anyone's way, so that no fault may be found with our ministry, but as servants of God we have commended ourselves in every way. We give in order that others may come and experience new life in Christ.

Offertory Praise

God of all, your love towards us is so marvelous. We thank you for all you have given us. We rejoice in this opportunity to be poor enough in spirit that we gladly share to make others part of your realm. We give because we recognize that we have nothing of ourselves, but with your great love for us we possess everything!

Benediction

Leader: The journey to Calvary begins.
People: We commend ourselves to God.
Leader: The journey calls us to receive the grace of God for every facet of our lives.
People: We commend ourselves to God.
Leader: The journey will call for great endurance on our part.
People: We commend ourselves to God.
Leader: Take the journey enfolded by Love, Truth, and Power. I commend us to God.
People: Hallelujah and amen!

THE FIRST SUNDAY OF LENT

Genesis 9:8–17
Psalm 25:1–10
1 Peter 3:18–22
Mark 1:9–15

Call to Worship

Leader: The Covenant God demands our accounting this day!
People: The Covenant Keeper is worthy of our praise!
Leader: The season of Lent recognizes the we are covenant breakers!
People: We are thankful that God always remembers and honors the covenant.
Leader: This is our day to remember.
People: We gather to be living signs of the covenant!

Call to Confession

God's covenant signs are visible in the clouds and rainbows that hover over our head. They are the reminders that we will not be destroyed by the flood waters ever again. Our confession is a sign to God that we have honest intent to honor the covenant we have made. Let us pray.

Confession

Steadfast and faithful God, we pause this day to confess our sin and to ask your forgiveness. We have gotten so caught up in the signs and symbols of earthly power that we fail to look up and remember you. Have mercy upon us, Great Lifter of Our Heads. In the name of the Christ, we pray.

Words of Assurance

Confession clears the way for restoration of our covenant with God. With steadfast love and tenderness God does remember us. This is good news.

Responsive Reading

Leader: God has our back!
People: This is certainly our hope and prayer. We have thrown in our lot with the Ancient of Days.

Leader: God, don't let us be embarrassed and dismissed.
People: God, don't allow the so-called "big dogs" to ride roughshod over us.
Leader: There are too many hoodlums waiting for our destruction.
People: There are plots and plans, snares and traps to put us to open shame.
Leader: God, we need to be schooled in ways of escape.
People: Teach us your truth. Lead us in your direction. Be our capable guide.
Leader: God, remember your homies. We are waiting on you to take them out.
People: The old folks told us their stories of how you worked on their behalf.
Leader: Don't let us down. In spite of our failures with you, because you love so hard, remember us.
People: God, we know that you are awesome and phat!
Leader: God, we are sure that you are all that!
People: Keep up your rep. Help us to ably represent you! We sincerely want to be your crew!

Offertory Invitation

For Christ also suffered for sins once for all, the righteous for the unrighteous, in order to bring us to God. He was put to death in the flesh but made alive in the spirit to bring us faultless before God. We cannot repay what we owe. Yet we can offer unto God our tangible thanks through tithes and offerings.

Offertory Praise

As our appeal to God for a good conscience, through the resurrection of Jesus Christ, who has gone into heaven and is at the right hand of God, with angels, authorities and powers made subject to him, we offer our monetary gifts. Receive them as a token of our gratitude. For we pray in the name of Love.

Benediction

Leader: Be love as you return to the world during Lent.
People: We will be love in our going out.
Leader: Be love as you return to the world during Lent.
People: We will be love in our coming in.
Leader: Be love as you return to the world during Lent.
People: We will be love in our leisure and at our work.
Leader: You are God's beloved children! Claim that power. Walk in that name!
People: Hallelujah and amen!

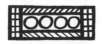

THE SECOND SUNDAY OF LENT

Genesis 17:1–7, 15–16
Psalm 22:23–31
Romans 4:13–25
Mark 8:31–38

Call to Worship

Leader: Court is in session. It is time for the reading of the will.
People: We have come to discover what we will receive from God.
Leader: The will has been established through Abraham and passed down to us.
People: God called Abram when he was old and promised succeeding generations.
Leader: The will is in order. We are exceedingly numerous.
People: The will is legal. We are exceedingly fruitful.
Leader: The will promised an established covenant between God and us.
People: Praise to the Almighty God for this living, ongoing, and faithful will!

Call to Confession

The reading of the will is only for the heirs of God who are in right standing with Jesus Christ. Sin breaks our relationshhip. Confession places us in the position to inherit eternal life.

Confession

God, all our feeble attempts to gain this world profit us nothing. And, in our flesh, we have sinned. Forgive us. Restore us to right standing with you. This we pray in the name of the One who gave us all.

Words of Assurance

Those who confess, repent, and seek to lose their lives for the sake of the gospel shall be saved. This is the assurance of God's will. Thanks be to God.

Responsive Reading

Leader: Give out a shout! The High God has kept every promise of the will.
People: This is a story worth telling. This is news that everyone needs to hear.
Leader: God has done it again. God stands by us when others count us out.
People: God's faithfulness is worthy of a praise report. God's love calls for celebration.
Leader: Those who are down and out, those who have been thrown to the curb, have a place with God.
People: God does not run away, avoid us, or keep us at arm's length.
Leader: It's time for us to pay up. The ledgers show that we owe God, big time!
People: From the ancestors, cheering from the balcony, to those generations yet unborn, God is faithful.
Leader: Power, glory, honor, and dominion belong to God.
People: We give up "hallelujah!" and shout out a call of "glory!" Our God is worthy to be praised!
Leader: God is in charge.
People: Among us, God has the last word!

Offertory Invitation

The promises of God rest on grace and are guaranteed to every descendant. We have received these great and precious promises. In order that others may know their covenant rights, let us share freely in the offering.

Offertory Praise

It was the faith of Abraham, as an old man, that made him able to receive God's promises. No distrust made him waver concerning the promises of God. But he grew in his faith as he gave glory to God, being fully convinced that God's promises would be kept. God, in this same faith, we give unto you today. For we offer these gifts in the name of the Promised Savior, Jesus the Christ.

Benediction

Leader: The service of resurrection is over. It's time to return to life in Lent.
People: We leave to be followers of Christ.

Leader: If you would be a follower, you must deny yourself, take up your cross, and walk the Jesus walk.

People: It is a hard thing that is demanded of us.

Leader: Indeed, what can you give in exchange for your life?

People: If we seek to save our lives, we will lose them.

Leader: Yet, if you live for the sake of the gospel, you shall be saved.

People: We return to Lent, unashamed of following Jesus.

Leader: Go, doing what Jesus would do! The power of every promise is yours.

People: Thanks be unto God for eternal victory!

THE THIRD SUNDAY OF LENT

Exodus 20:1–17
Psalm 19
1 Corinthians 1:18–25
John 2:13–22

Call to Worship

Leader: This day we encounter a speaking God.
People: Speak, God. Your servants are listening.
Leader: As a matter of fact, our God uses many words to communicate with us.
People: Speak God. Your servants want to hear.
Leader: The Ten Commandments are not simple rules or nice suggestions, but ways of conducting our lives.
People: You have already spoken, God! Give us grace, now, to hear and to obey.

Call to Confession

God has called "do not" and we have done. God has decreed "do" and we have not. This is our time of getting right with the One who has already given the commands. Let's confess our sin of both omission and commission.

Confession

Holy One, you are God, Sovereign over all. You have commanded and we have disobeyed. You have given orders and we have failed to heed them. You have set the limits and we have tried to establish our own boundaries and to make our own way. Forgive us our sin. Make us holy. Be our God, we pray, through Jesus Christ.

Words of Assurance

It is always God's delight to deliver us from the many Egypts of our lives. Our slavery to sin has been canceled. With our confession we are in right relationship to the Deliverer of Zion. This is good news!

Responsive Reading

Leader: The whole universe sends out a shout for the Majestic One.

People: There is not a spot where the glory of God does not give out a yell.

Leader: The splendor of every day is the signature of the Divine Designer.

People: The awesome darkness of the night signals the wonders of God's knowledge.

Leader: Without the limitation of articulation and not needing the noise of speech, the glory of God is shouted throughout the world.

People: The heavens establish the dwelling of the Most High God. Like a powerful sprinter the sun radiates over the whole world.

Leader: From the rising of the sun till the going down of the same, the glory of the Lord is evident.

People: God's laws are perfect. They will keep us living large.

Leader: God's decrees are not difficult. They will make us wise.

People: God's judgments are right. They bring joy to our hearts.

Leader: God's commandments are not simple wishes. They save our lives.

People: Reverence for God has kept us all the days of our existence.

Leader: Respect for the High God has always been the aim of the ancestors.

People: Loving God, following after God, and doing the will of God is better than all else.

Leader: Loving God, following after God, and doing the will of God brings all else unto us.

People: God is sweeter than honey in the comb.

Leader: God is better to have than money.

People: When we keep God's ways and walk in God's Word, we discover great rewards.

Leader: Keep God's Word and sin will never have power over you.

People: We will keep God's Word so that we might be found faultless before God's throne in the judgment. Let the words of our mouth and the meditations of our heart be acceptable unto you, O Lord, our rock and our redeemer.

Offertory Invitation

The message about the cross is foolishness to those who are perishing. But to us who are being saved it is the power of God. Let us share from our resources in order that others might come to know this saving power.

Offertory Praise

God, you decided that through the foolishness of preaching salvation would spread to those who believe. Accept these our gifts, that the foolishness of the cross might continue to be spread.

We pray in the name of Jesus, who died on the cross and rose again.

Benediction

Leader: Leave to be signs of the power of the cross.
People: We are the temples of the Holy Spirit, resurrected to new life in Jesus.
Leader: Leave to be signs of the power of the cross.
People: We are people of God who will be knocked down, but will rise again.
Leader: Leave to be signs of the power of the cross.
People: We believe in the power of God to raise us to new life, despite any circumstances.
Leader: God, the Power, Jesus the Redeemer, and the Holy Spirit will keep you on your way. Go, being signs of the cross.
People: Hallelujah and amen.

THE FOURTH SUNDAY OF LENT

Numbers 21:4–9
Psalm 107:1–3, 17–22
Ephesians 2:1–10
John 3:14–21

Call to Worship

Leader: The Redeeming God, who has delivered us from every snake pit, calls us to gather.
People: The snakes have been vicious; their venom has been deadly. We need to be revived.
Leader: The Delivering God, who calls us to look up and be saved, is present for healing.
People: We detest being miserable. We long to be made whole. Let's worship the God of our salvation.

Call to Confession

When the snakes are biting and death seems a viable way of escape, we begin to fret and to complain. In our impatience we sin against God. Again, this day we have opportunity to confess our sin. Let us pray.

Confession

God, we have sinned by speaking against those who have hurt us and even against you. We pray this morning that you would take away every serpent in our life and forgive us our sin. Cleanse us and make us whole, we pray in the name of Jesus, who was lifted up for our salvation.

Words of Assurance

For God so loved the world that the Only Begotten Son has been lifted up for our sin. Everyone who believes shall be saved. My sisters and brothers, this is good news. Thanks be unto God.

Responsive Reading

Leader: It's time to make noise in here! The love of God has sustained us another week.

People: It's time for us to raise the roof with our thanksgiving. For God has been mighty good.

Leader: Let the redeemed of God say so! If you have been delivered from troubles this week, give out a shout.

People: Praise God!

Leader: If you have known healing in your body or if God has touched someone because you prayed, it's time to give it up for God.

People: God, we praise you!

Leader: If God has provided food on your tables and kept the bill collectors from repossessing what you have, this is the time to let God know your gratitude.

People: Great God, we lift your name on high.

Leader: If God has answered your prayers, saved you from distress, and stayed the hand of death on your behalf, you owe God big-time praise.

People: Bless your matchless name, God of Benefits.

Leader: God's Word has been sent to heal and to deliver. If the Word has blessed you in any way this past week, let's hear it for the Living Word of hope.

People: God, we praise you for your steadfast love and your wonderful works. We offer you the sacrifice of thanksgiving with the fruit of our lips. We will tell of your deeds with loud songs of joy throughout the coming week. It's mighty good to know you, God, and we magnify your most holy name!

Offertory Invitation

For by grace we have been saved through faith, and this is not our own doing, it is the gift of God. It's not of our works so that we might boast. For what we are, God has made us to be, created in Christ Jesus for good works. Our way of living is to return a portion of what we have been so lavishly given. Let us share freely.

Offertory Praise

God, you are so rich in mercy. It is by your great love, which you have given us, even when we were dead through our trespasses, that you have made us alive with Christ. By grace we have been saved and raised to sit with him in heavenly places. Please receive these gifts as a token of the immeasurable riches you have given us in generous kindness. We pray in the name of the Gift Above Every Gift.

Benediction

Leader: Just as Moses lifted up the serpent in the wilderness, so must the Son of God be lifted up by our lives in the world.
People: Whosoever believes in the Son of God may have eternal life.
Leader: Go and spread this good news.
People: We leave to live this good news by our lives!
Leader: God the Giver, Jesus Christ the gift, and the Holy Spirit, the Power, will keep you.
People: Hallelujah and amen.

THE FIFTH SUNDAY OF LENT

Jeremiah 31:31–34
Psalm 51:1–12 or Psalm 119:9–16
Hebrews 5:5–10
John 12:20–33

Call to Worship

Leader: The Writing God has called us to assemble.
People: Our hearts are open that God may write afresh upon them.
Leader: The Covenant God wants to write with indelible ink the way to eternal life.
People: God wrote the covenant. We continue to break the covenant. We long for refreshing.
Leader: God has promised to write the covenant upon the tablets of our hearts.
People: Worship is covenant refresher time. Let the writing begin.

Call to Confession

In the days of his flesh, Jesus offered up prayers and supplications with loud cries and tears, to the one who was able to save him from death, and he was heard because of his reverent submission. Although he was the Son of God, he learned obedience through what he suffered in order that the Great Eraser might go to work. Let us pray.

Confession

Create in me a clean heart, O God, and put a right spirit within me. Do not cast me away from your presence. Forgive my sin and do not take your Holy Spirit from me. Restore to me the joy of your salvation, and sustain in me a willing spirit. Hear our prayers, through Christ we pray.

Words of Assurance

God has promised that, "They shall all know me, from the least of them to the greatest. . . . for I will forgive their iniquity and remember their sin no more." This is our good news!

Responsive Reading

Leader: Mercy! Mercy! Mercy!

People: We have heard our ancestors pray this prayer.

Leader: Mercy! Mercy! Mercy!

People: Today this is our sincere petition.

Leader: God's mercy is well known and much necessary.

People: God's mercy is born of God's love. It is God's mercy that blots out our sin.

Leader: God's mercy washes from us our hidden sin, and cleanses us from damnation.

People: We have sinned and done evil. God's judgment would be just. But we plead for mercy.

Leader: Mercy! Mercy! Mercy!

People: From birth, our tendency has been rebellion. God's mercy allows wisdom to teach us new ways.

Leader: God's mercy will purge us, cleanse us, and restore us to relationship with the Ancient of Days.

People: God, don't hide your face from us. Your mercy is what we need.

Leader: Put on the joy of God's mercy. Let the glad sounds of gladness ring from your lips.

People: Mercy! Mercy! Mercy! God's encore brings shouts of redemption from formerly crushed spirits. God's mercy restores our souls and sustains us with a willing spirit. Thank God for mercy.

Offertory Invitation

Those who love their life will lose it. And those who hate their life in this world will keep it for eternity. Whoever follows Jesus must follow him in the ministry of sacrificial giving. This is our time.

Offertory Praise

Jesus has declared, "And I, when I am lifted up from the earth, will draw all people to myself." God, we thank you for the privilege of looking up and receiving new life. Use these our gifts to assist others to look and to live. In the name of the Christ we pray.

Benediction

Leader: The crowds asked the disciples to see Jesus. The world yet wants to see the Christ.

People: We leave to be images of the Risen Christ in the places we will touch this week.

Leader: The crowds were oppressed, afflicted, and in despair. In hopeful anticipation they said, "We wish to see Jesus."

People: We leave to be those who will advocate on behalf of the oppressed, to relieve afflictions and to be agents of hope in the midst of the world's despair.

Leader: Go in the power of the Transforming God, the Redeeming Christ, and the Comforter. Be a Christ figure to a needy world.

The commission is ours!

THE SIXTH SUNDAY OF LENT · PALM SUNDAY

Mark 11:1–11 or John 12:12–16
Psalm 118:1–2, 19–29
Isaiah 50:4–9a
Psalm 31:9–16
Philippians 2:5–11
Mark 14:1–15:47

Call to Worship

Leader: The Lord of Need summons us this day.
People: What can we possibly give to the All-Sufficient One?
Leader: The Lord of Need asks for our participation in the unfolding drama of salvation.
People: What do we have to bring to the Supplier of Every Need?
Leader: Jesus sent the disciples to untie and bring a never-ridden colt for his use.
People: We have gifts we have never released, talents lying dormant, and hopes still unborn.
Leader: This is the day. This is the place. The Lord who needs us is calling.

Call to Confession

God has called for all we have to be released for use. The question becomes, "What are you doing?" Unless we have given our all to the One who is requesting, it is mandatory that we pause to confess our sin.

Confession

God, we love a good parade. We dress up. We join in waving our leafy branches. We even call out a loud, "Hosanna!" Then, we go back to business as usual. Forgive us our sin. Use us for your great glory, we pray in the name of the Christ.

Words of Assurance

With our confession, sin is wiped away and restoration is ours. This is good news.

Responsive Reading

Leader: God, where are you? We're in over our head!

People: Our sadness is unending. Our souls are filled with anguish. We need your help.

Leader: God, we have lived lives of difficulty. Sorrow seems to be our constant theme. Before we can catch our breath and recover from one blow, another issue comes to push us back.

People: Those who hate us and plot against us are rejoicing at our plight. Our world neighbors avoid us as if our condition is contagious. Even our so-called liberal friends dodge us, not knowing what else to say or to do.

Leader: The hard drive of our mind is filled to capacity! It's overwhelming and complex, trying to figure a way out of ugly situations.

People: We feel like precious, fragile vessels that have been dropped and shattered.

Leader: We have been embarrassed due to wrongful gossip about us everywhere. Plots of destruction are legend. They feel this is a good time to wipe us off and even wipe us out!

People: But our times are in your hands. We put our trust in you. You are our God and have been our God from before the beginning!

Leader: Deliver us from every enemy.

People: Let your face shine upon us. Save us in your steadfast love.

Offertory Invitation

The Sovereign God has given us the tongue of teachers, so that we may know how to sustain the weary with our words. Morning by morning we awaken with ears alert to be taught of God. For this reason, we share so that others might come to hear and to know.

Offertory Praise

Gracious God, you have helped us and we have not been disgraced. Our faces are set like flint. Because of your help we offer these gifts back to you. Let them bless others, is our prayer, in the name of the Helper of the Helpless.

Benediction

Leader: The parade of palms is finished.

People: Hosannas are silent. The crowds have walked away.

Leader: During this week, someone will betray the Savior.

People: Jesus, is it I?

Leader: Go, following the footsteps of Jesus to Calvary. The keeping power of the Holy Spirit goes with you. This will be a holy week of suffering, tears, and pain. But it is ours to remember, that Resurrection Sunday is on the way!

People: Thanks be to God! Hallelujah and amen.

HOLY WEEK

This period of walking with Jesus to Calvary is not a usual and customary tradition in African American congregations. However, this is a prime evangelistic opportunity to reach out to your surrounding community with a soup and salad lunch followed by a short meditative worship experience. There are un-churched, previously churched, and out-of-the-area churched people who need to spend a few moments as we march toward Holy Thursday, Good Friday, and Easter. The readings signal what of significance was happening to Jesus and the disciples during this last week of their ministry together.

Instead of using the Psalms as a responsive reading, I have provided a litany based upon the travels of Jesus. Following the readings, it may be helpful to provide a few moments of silence for personal reflection and meditation.

This period of walking with Jesus to Calvary is one to engage those not usually involved in the "busy life" of the congregation. Pulling together men and women who are retired to prepare the soup and salad each day gives ample opportunity for community building. Another suggestion would be to have this type of worship during each week of Lent. You may be pleasantly surprised at who will show up to a noon worship experience. Offering plates should be placed at the rear of the sanctuary and simply mentioned after the benediction. What monies are received will offset the cost of food and kitchen supplies. A particular mission in your local community can become the focus of any "additional" funds received.

Target schools, businesses, doctors' offices, and the area within a six-block radius of your building to leave flyers announcing lunch and meditation with a "free will offering." If your mission's work area is already involved with a local outreach project, mention it in your publicity. Some people who attend no congregation will be glad to give to "charity." Your church gets the credit and earns "brownie points" for caring. Invite those who "brown bag" for lunch to come and share the worship time with others as we journey to Calvary. Make this a meaningful occasion for Christ to touch hearts!

MONDAY OF HOLY WEEK

Isaiah 42:1–9
Psalm 36:5–11
Hebrews 9:11–15
John 12:1–11

Call to Worship

Leader: Here is my servant, whom I uphold, my chosen, in whom my soul delights.
People: God's spirit is upon him. Jesus will bring forth justice to the nations.
Leader: He will not cry or lift up his voice or make it heard in the street.
People: A bruised reed he will not break, and a dimly burning wick he will not quench.
Leader: Jesus will not grow faint or be crushed.
People: He is preparing to establish justice in the earth. We walk with him this week.

Call to Confession

The steadfast love of our God extends to the heavens. God's faithfulness is beyond the clouds. Our confession allows us the ability to take refuge in the shadow of God's wings. Let us pray.

Confession

The blood of goats and heifers will not satisfy the sacrifice required for us. We thank you, God, for the blood of Jesus Christ, who entered once for all into the Holy Place. Forgive us our sin. In the name of Love we pray. Amen.

Responsive Reading

Leader: Monday is the day of Jesus Christ's anointing.
People: The grateful dead were present.
Leader: Lazarus had already experienced resurrection.
People: The ungrateful thief was present.

Leader: Judas had his eye on what could be stolen.
People: Jesus was present.
Leader: And a woman anointed him as King.
People: She poured the anointing oil on his head as on a high priest.
Leader: She knelt down and worshiped at his feet.
People: The fragrance of her expensive ointment filled the room.
Leader: Instead of using the ointment for her own burial, she poured it all on Jesus.
People: The poor were present. They are yet among us. Jesus noticed them.
Leader: Her anointing prepared Jesus for the cross that was ahead.
People: A great crowd was present watching the sights, but not worshiping.
Leader: We gather to worship. We will walk with Jesus during this week of holy days.

Silence for meditation and personal reflection

Benediction

Leader: Christ is the mediator of a new covenant.
People: We have been called to a new inheritance because of the sacrifice of Jesus.
Leader: Go in peace! Amen.

TUESDAY OF HOLY WEEK

Isaiah 49:1–7
Psalm 71:1–14
1 Corinthians 1:18–31
John 12:20–36

Call to Worship

Leader: Why have you gathered?
People: We want to see Jesus!
Leader: The Light is with us for only a little longer.
People: We will walk in the light.

Call to Confession

On this second day of Holy Week, as we walk toward Calvary, let us confess before God.

Confession

Loving God, the message of the cross is foolishness to those who are perishing, but to us who are being saved it is the power of God. Forgive us our sin. Fill us with the power to follow you.

Words of Assurance

God is never far from us. The words of our confession draw us closer to the heart of God. This is good news.

Responsive Reading

Leader: The hour is coming closer. The appointed time is near.
People: Unless a grain of wheat falls to the earth and dies, it remains just a single grain.
Leader: But if it dies, it bears much fruit.
People: Those who love their life lose it. And those who hate their life in this world will keep it for eternal life.

Leader: Whoever serves Jesus must follow. For where Jesus goes, we must go also.

People: Now my soul is troubled! And what should we say?

Leader: It was for this reason that Jesus was born to die.

People: God will get the glory.

Leader: And the world will be judged.

People: The ruler of this world will be driven out.

Leader: And Jesus will be lifted up for all the world to see.

People: We walk with Jesus to Calvary.

Silence for meditation and personal reflection

Benediction

Leader: If you walk in the darkness you do not know where you are going.

People: We leave to walk in the light. We are children of light.

Leader: The Light is with you a little longer. Go in peace!

WEDNESDAY OF HOLY WEEK

Isaiah 50:4–9a
Psalm 70
Hebrews 12:1–3
John 13:21–32

Call to Worship

Leader: God has given us tongues that we might teach others.
People: God calls us to sustain the weary with our meager words.
Leader: Morning by morning God gives us alert ears.
People: God has opened our ears so we may be taught.
Leader: When we do not rebel and turn from God, we will be used in ministry to the world.
People: Let us stand up together. The Lord, our God, is our constant help.

Call to Confession

God is pleased to deliver us. We only need to ask forgiveness for our sin.

Confession

Gracious God, we have been rebellious and turned away from you. We have fallen into sin and brought disgrace to our witness. Forgive us our sin. Deliver us. Set our face like flint so that we might see no evil, hear no evil, and do no evil in your sight. Declare us "not guilty" in order that we may serve you in the world.

Words of Assurance

Therefore, since we are surrounded by so great a cloud of witnesses, let us also lay aside every weight and the sin that clings so closely, and let us run with perseverance the race that is set before us, looking to Jesus, the pioneer and perfecter of our faith, who for the sake of the joy that was set before him endured the cross, disregarding its shame, and has taken his seat at the right hand of the throne of God. Consider him who endured such hostility against himself from sinners, so that you may not grow weary or lose heart. My sisters and brothers, this is certainly good news!

Responsive Reading

Leader: The Teacher became a mother one night.
People: Jesus prepared his children a meal. He used his own body and his own blood.
Leader: The Great One became a mother one night.
People: Jesus prepared his children a bath and washed their dirty feet.
Leader: The Parent became sad one night.
People: After preparing and serving, washing and wishing, he knew betrayal was close at hand.
Leader: Jesus said, "Very truly, I tell you, one of you will betray me."
People: John asked, "Lord, who is it?"
Leader: That question continues to ring loud among us today.
People: We ask, "Lord, is it me?"

Silence for meditation and personal reflection

Benediction

Leader: We are walking with Jesus to Calvary.
People: Who among us will betray the Sovereign of Creation?
Leader: Go in peace!

HOLY THURSDAY

In the black Church this night has been deemed appropriate for the washing of feet. It is an old custom that seems to have lost its appeal in recent generations. Yet the Savior washed the feet of his disciples on this sacred night. And we can return to this tradition, which indicates humility and service to another. If feet washing is not desired, some sort of hand washing ritual may be exchanged, with lotion provided to conclude our act of care. It is also the night that the Passover Meal is celebrated. This meal is the one eaten just before the children of Israel began their exodus from slavery in Egypt. As they were to be busy packing up and preparing for the signal to move out, the meal was to be eaten while the participants were on alert. On this night, Holy Thursday, the congregation could be asked to pack the typical meal that our ancestors might have packed as they were preparing for moving out under the cover of night for freedom. Brought in picnic baskets, this meal is a prime opportunity to celebrate together and to covenant anew to be community for each other.

Call to Worship
(Exodus 12:1–14)

Song of Celebration

Call to Sharing a Meal
The feast of the slave community has always held a special place in our hearts. We can easily remember Granny packing the basket as we made ready to travel to worship, to a quilting bee, or simply to spend time with our kin. As we migrated from the south to the north and midwest, we can recall with fondness the many brown bags, packed with fried chicken, homemade rolls, deviled eggs, fried pies, and potato salad that traveled with us, in trains, buses and cars. These meals sustained us in times that the dining cars didn't welcome us. Eating together has been part of our salvation. The Jewish community has its meal, which Jesus celebrated with his friends. In that same spirit, tonight we will open our picnic baskets around the tables and share with our friends. Freedom is on the way. Let's be ready to heed its call.

Table Grace

God, you continue to call us to make haste for freedom. We thank you for your call. As we gather around these tables in celebration of the awesome ministry of Jesus to and with his friends, help us to remember his servant attitude. He prepared and served a meal. He washed the feet of his friends and affirmed them. Help us to follow his example on this holy night. Bless the abundance of food that has been prepared and that we will eat. Bless each hand that touched it in order that it grace our tables. Bless those folks with little and those with none tonight. Bless those folks who are yet willingly shackled in bondage. Sanctify this food as nourishment for our bodies. And when we leave this place, let its nutrition energize us enough to work towards the day when the world can gather around banquet tables like these with thanksgiving. In the name of Jesus Christ we pray. Amen.

After Supper Response

Congregational song of praise

Scripture Reading

(John 13:1–7, 31b–35)

Invitation to Servanthood

Love is an action verb. Our foreparents washed each other's feet as a sign of love, care, and service. Tonight we will offer a similar sign by washing each other's hands. Handiwipes are available at each table. After each one has cleaned another's hand, let us take the time to put lotion on that same pair of hands. Then let us pray for the ministry opportunities before our neighbors.

Hymn of Praise

Call to Communion

(1 Corinthians 11:23–26)
Communion is served.

Benediction

(Read responsively Psalm 116:1–2, 12–19.)
Leader: Go in peace to love God and to serve your neighbors in all that you do.
People: Amen and amen.

GOOD FRIDAY

This worship experience is an alternative to the preaching style commonly used. This can be a worship of scripture and songs appropriate to the Word Jesus speaks. It is a time when lay speakers, young and senior, can participate in meaningful ways.

The sanctuary is dark as the congregation gathers. Acolytes enter and light altar candles. The processional of the male choir is next, followed by their a cappella singing of an appropriate spiritual. When they are finished and seated, the spotlight follows Jesus and Simon, slowly coming up the aisle bearing the cross. It is laid against pulpit where it is very visible.

Call to Worship

(Isaiah 52:13–53:12)
Jesus and Simon leave as congregation stands to sing. (Music selected by musicians)

Invocation

On this most sacred night we gather to remember. We remember the greatest sacrifice of love. We remember the journey of Jesus to the cross. We remember the price Jesus paid for our salvation. And we remember our sinfulness. We remember that his disciples ran away afraid. We remember that Jesus was left alone. Tonight, we gather to be present. Gracious God, this night, we gather to remember. Thank you for Jesus. Thank you for your presence. Thank you for your love. Thank you for this holy memory. For the sake of Jesus Christ we pray. Amen.

Scripture

(Hebrews 10:16–25 or Hebrews 4:14-16; 5:7–9)

Congregational Hymn

Seven Last Words of Jesus: The First Word
(Luke 23:26–38) *Father Forgive Them*

Solo

Seven Last Words of Jesus: The Second Word
(Luke 23:39–43) *Today You Are With Me*

Congregational Hymn

Seven Last Words of Jesus: The Third Word
(John 19:25–27) *Woman, Behold Thy Son*

The Male Chorus

Seven Last Words of Jesus: The Fourth Word
(John 19:28) *I Thirst*

Congregational Hymn

Seven Last Words of Jesus: The Fifth Word
(Psalm 22) *My God, My God, Why?*

Solo

Seven Last Words of Jesus: The Sixth Word
(Luke 23:44–46) *Into Thy Hands*

The Male Chorus

Seven Last Words of Jesus: The Seventh Word
(John 19:29–30) *It Is Finished!*

The pastor invites all musical participants to the altar. Each one is given a nail for the cross. Sound effects, offstage, enlarge the sound of pounding.

The pastor invites the congregation to the altar as ushers hand out nails for taking home to remember this significant night. (Congregation can bring offering forward as they come to kneel and pray.) When the last person leaves the altar, the music ceases.

When all have finished, in silence the communion stewards strip the altar. The lights are turned off with the exception of a spotlight on the cross. There is a space of silence. The pastor instructs the congregation to leave in thanksgiving and silence. There is no additional music or talking.

HOLY SATURDAY

Call to Worship

Leader: Each of us is born.
People: Our days are too short and filled with trouble.
Leader: We come up like a flower and we wither.
People: Like a fleeting shadow we do not last.
Leader: Our days are determined.
People: Our death is certain.
Leader: Yesterday, death claimed Jesus!
People: A funeral procession followed his body to a borrowed tomb.
Leader: It is not the end of the story.
People: Thanks be to God.

Call to Confession

Mortals die. Jesus died. He was ready, prepared, and able to say, "It is finished!" Our confession helps us to stay prepared to meet death. Let us pray.

Confession

In you, O God, we seek refuge; do not let us ever be put to shame. Forgive our sin. In your righteousness, deliver us from the bonds of death. Incline your ears to us. Rescue speedily. Be our rock of refuge and our strong fortress of salvation. Our times are in your hand. In the name of the Savior we pray.

Words of Assurance

God's face shines upon us when we confess our sin. It is with steadfast love that we are forgiven and made whole. This is good news.

Responsive Reading

Leader: A wealthy but secret disciple, Joseph of Arimathea, received the body of Jesus for burial.
People: Lord, where were your vocal followers?

Leader: Pilate allowed a secret disciple to take the wrapped body of a dead Jesus and lay it in a borrowed tomb.
People: Lord, where were your vocal followers?
Leader: A great stone was rolled in front of the door to seal the tomb. The funeral procession was very small. There were three women and one man, a disciple, at the funeral.
People: Lord, where were your vocal followers?
Leader: The chief priests and the Pharisees gathered before Pilate to plot.
People: Lord, where were your vocal followers?
Leader: They decided to put guards all around the tomb to keep Jesus locked inside a grave.
People: Lord, where were your vocal followers?
Leader: The women followers sat silent, opposite the tomb, preparing to do their last act of loving ministry to a dead corpse at the proper time.
People: Jesus died. His followers did not remember his words of assurance that he would rise. Today the whole world waits as Jesus lies in a tomb.
Leader: Lord, where are your vocal followers?

Silence

Benediction

Leader: Go into the world! Be a vocal disciple. Tell the world that resurrection will raise the dead! Tell it everywhere you go!
People: Hallelujah and amen!

6 · THE EASTER SEASON

The resurrection is about our ability to rise! Jesus was tormented, mocked, caused public shame, and ultimately killed. Evil felt it had the final word. Death considered itself a victor. The grave thought itself, "the end." But Jesus got up! Evil's chain was broken. Death's hold was denied. The grave was forced to release its captive. God's power was evidenced as Jesus, the Christ, rose from the grave.

The resurrection is about our ability to be like Jesus Christ and to rise! We rise above evil circumstances. We rise above the death of hopes and dreams. We rise above our graves of depression, desolation, and despair. Every Sunday worship experience is another celebration of the resurrection. Getting up and beginning again is our theme song of joyous and unending praise.

EASTER SUNDAY

Acts 10:34–43
Psalm 118:1–2, 14–24
1 Corinthians 15:1–11
John 20:1–18

Call to Worship

Leader: Christ the Sovereign God is risen!
People: Christ the Sovereign God is risen indeed!
Leader: We celebrate the God of Life!
People: We give praise to the God who conquered death.
Leader: We bless God, who took the victory away from hell.
People: We worship God, who won for us eternal life!
Leader: We have a story to tell.
People: New life begins again. Jesus Christ the Sovereign God is risen indeed!

Call to Confession

God shows no partiality, but anyone who shows reverence and does what is right is acceptable. With our confession we join the God of Life.

Confession

God, the message of Jesus has spread, beginning in Galilee. With the power of the Holy Spirit Jesus went about doing good and healing all who were oppressed by evil. Too often we have participated in the oppression of powerlessness and we have refused to do the good that we know. Forgive us our sin. Grant us new life, we pray in the name of him who rose victorious from the dead.

Words of Assurance

All the prophets testify about him that everyone who believes in Jesus Christ receives forgiveness of sins through his name. This is our salvation. Thanks be to God.

Responsive Reading

Leader: God has done it again!

People: It's been a long journey to new life.

Leader: But God has done it again!

People: Fridays are deadly, but the day of resurrection does come!

Leader: God has done it again!

People: For every closed eye is not sleeping, and every good-bye ain't gone!

Leader: God has done it again!

People: For evil thought Jesus was down and out, but death was only a comma, not God's period!

Leader: God has done it again!

People: We are an Easter people and rising is always our theme of praise.

Leader: God has done it again!

People: The impossible has been made possible. The unthinkable is visible.

Leader: God has done it again!

People: We shall not die, but we shall live and give glory to God with our deeds.

Leader: God has done it again!

People: The gates of righteousness have been opened for us.

Leader: God has done it again!

People: The stone that the builders rejected has become the chief cornerstone.

Leader: This is the Lord's doing and it's marvelous in our eyes. This is the day the Lord has made. We will rejoice and be glad in it.

People: For God has done it again!

Offertory Invitation

We have been handed down that which we have received. Christ died for our sins in accordance with the scriptures, was buried, and was raised on the third day. This news is worth our sharing. Our gifts will keep the message spreading to new generations.

Offertory Praise

God, it is by your amazing grace that we are what we are today. Your grace toward us has not been in vain. We recognize that it was not of our own capabilities, but your divine ability to pursue us, that brought us unto you. Our gifts are simply a meager attempt to say thanks. We offer them in the Name of Love.

Benediction

Leader: Leave with a message upon your lips.
People: I have seen the Risen Christ!
Leader: Leave with a message upon your hearts.
People: I have seen the Risen Christ!
Leader: Leave with a message being your life.
People: I have seen the Risen Christ!
Leader: He is risen!
People: Christ the Sovereign One is risen indeed!
Leader: Go in that faith-filled power to love God and to serve your neighbor in all that you do!
People: Hallelujah and amen.

THE SECOND SUNDAY OF EASTER

Acts 4:32–35
Psalm 133
1 John 1:1–2:2
John 20:19–31

Call to Worship

Leader: The Resurrecting God is present.
People: We have been dead in trespasses and sin.
Leader: The God of new life is here.
People: We are stormy weather people, seeking the Son!
Leader: God seeks those who believe that fresh starts belong to them.
People: With believing hearts, willing minds, and expectant spirits we offer the God of Resurrection praise.

Call to Confession

Many believed in the Jesus of the resurrection and were one of one heart and soul. With great power and conviction they gave their testimony of Jesus Christ, and great grace was upon them all. For our witness to be effective, our lives must be right with God. Confession clears the way.

Confession

Generous Spirit, we have believed that there was too little to go around. We have practiced the ministry of scarcity. We have felt that, surely, you didn't have enough to go around, and we have tried to hoard what we had. It is the message of the world, that those who have are those who get! We have believed their lies. Forgive us the sin that separates us from you. Restore us to fellowship with you.

Words of Assurance

Little children, we have been given God's Word that we may not sin. But, when we do sin, we have an advocate, Jesus Christ the righteous. He is the atoning sacrifice for our sins, and not for ours only but also for the sins of the whole world. This is our good news!

Responsive Reading

Leader: This is a family reunion!

People: The elders are in the house and the little ones are present too.

Leader: This is a wonderful family reunion!

People: There is no love like that of kinfolks. The support of family is essential.

Leader: This is an awesome family reunion!

People: During the week, while we are apart, it's easy to feel alone and even isolated.

Leader: But in this place, during this time, we know that others have our back!

People: This is family reunion at its best!

Offertory Invitation

When the Church was formed there were no needy people among them, for as many owned land or houses sold them and brought the proceeds of what was sold to distribute among all. Today, God only requires that we be cheerful givers. For when we share there is enough for all.

Offertory Praise

God, we have given according to your Word. The life of Jesus Christ has been revealed unto us. We have seen it and testify to its revelation in our lives. We offer these tokens in order that others may become part of this family so your joy may be complete. Receive them in the name of the Giver of New Life.

Benediction

Leader: Peace be with you!

People: And peace be multiplied with you!

Leader: Receive the Holy Spirit!

People: Let it breathe upon us again!

Leader: The call of God, the shalom of Christ, and the peace of the Holy Spirit are ours!

People: Thanks be unto the God of Resurrection! Amen.

THE THIRD SUNDAY OF EASTER

Acts 3:12–19
Psalm 4
1 John 3:1–7
Luke 24:36–48

Call to Worship

Leader: The pull-up God is ready to offer a hand.
People: We need the presence of One who will lift us this day.
Leader: The hands-up God wants to arrest your attention.
People: We long for the consideration of One who will provide for us another chance.
Leader: The Author of Life is offering opportunities for those who want to write new chapters in the Book of Life.
People: We have gathered to begin all over again. Let the fresh words be written upon our hearts.

Call to Confession

Friends, in the past week we have acted in ignorance. Yet God has promised, "Repent, therefore, and turn to God that your sin may be wiped out." This time of confession is ours to get it right with God! Let us pray.

Confession

Righteous Judge, everyone who commits sin is guilty of lawlessness. And we have broken your law. We know that Jesus was revealed to take away sin, and in him there is no sin. Forgive us our sin and restore us, we pray, in the name of the Risen Christ.

Words of Assurance

See what love God has given us, that we should be called children of God. With our confession, that is what we are. Beloved, we are God's children now! This is our blessed assurance!

Responsive Reading

Leader: God, I know you hear us calling you!

People: The way life is cutting up makes it seem as if you have backed all the way up and left us alone.

Leader: We are involved in a full-scale pity party. For we know that you hear us calling you!

People: The time for hurt feelings and whimpering has past. We need you to come and see about us.

Leader: God, I know you hear us calling you!

People: Our pouting dishonors you. Our poked out lips bring shame to your name. Where are you?

Leader: God, I know you hear us calling you!

People: Perhaps our calling is in vain!

Leader: When we are disturbed, it is best to shut up! In this way we do not sin.

People: Could silence be a proper sacrifice to show God our trust?

Leader: Praise evokes the presence of God. Whining won't make the face of God shine!

People: God, we will lie down and ponder your wonders in our life. Allow us to sleep in peace. For God, by our trust, we know that you hear us calling unto you!

Offertory Invitation

Jesus' question to the disciples after the resurrection was, "Do you have anything here to eat?" The disciples were caught off guard and the reality helped them to see Jesus more clearly. It is not in what we have that we see Jesus. It is in what we share that others see the reality of the Risen Christ. Let us give with a spirit of generosity.

Offertory Praise

Jesus opened the minds of the disciples to understand the scriptures. Please accept these gifts as our comprehension that it is indeed far better to give than to receive. Bless both the gifts and the givers, we pray in the name of the Messiah.

Benediction

Leader: The Messiah had to suffer, to die, to be buried, and to rise from the dead on the third day.

People: He did it that repentance and forgiveness of sin would be proclaimed in his name to all nations.

Leader: We are the witnesses of these things.

People: He lives! He lives! Christ Jesus lives in us! We leave to tell the world!

Leader: The Power, the Redemption, and the Glory go before us!

People: May it be so today and forever!

THE FOURTH SUNDAY OF EASTER

Acts 4:5–12
Psalm 23
1 John 3:16–24
John 10:11–18

Call to Worship

Leader: The Name above All Names is taking attendance!
People: We have gathered in the power of the Matchless Name.
Leader: There is wonder working-power in that name.
People: There is redemption and salvation in that name.
Leader: There is healing and comfort for the disconsolate in that name.
People: Jesus Christ, the sweetest name of all, is present to us. There is no other name under heaven by which we can be saved. We worship in his name!

Call to Confession

The Good Shepherd has laid down his life for the sheep. With our sin we have strayed away. Let us confess together.

Confession

We know love by this—that Jesus laid down his life for us—and we ought to lay down our lives for one another. Instead we bite and devour each other. God, forgive us our sin. Restore us to active love. We pray in the name of the One who loved us enough to pay our penalty.

Words of Assurance

The Good Shepherd has laid down his life for us. He knows his own. There is one flock. With our confession, we have one Shepherd. This is good news.

Responsive Reading

Leader: The Lord is my Shepherd. I shall not want.
People: This is our confidence.
Leader: He makes me lie down in green pastures.
People: This is our restoration.
Leader: He leads me besides the still waters. He restores my soul.

People: This is our healing.

Leader: He leads me in right paths for his name's sake.

People: This is our direction and security.

Leader: Even though I walk through the valley of death, I fear no evil. You are with me.

People: This is our faith.

Leader: Your rod and your staff comfort me.

People: This is our blessed assurance.

Leader: You prepare a table before me in the presence of my enemies.

People: This is our delightful feast.

Leader: You anoint my head with oil.

People: This is our consecration.

Leader: My cup overflows.

People: This is our abundance.

Leader: Surely goodness and mercy shall follow me all the days of my life.

People: And we shall dwell in the house of the Lord throughout eternity. This is our good news.

Offertory Invitation

We know love by this, that Jesus laid down his life for us. How does God's love abide in anyone who has the world's goods and sees a brother or sister in need and yet refuses to help? Little children, let us love, not in word or speech, but in truth and in our acts of giving.

Offertory Praise

God, we have boldness before you and have received abundance from you. We have obeyed your commandment to share with the world. We offer these gifts in faithful obedience, through the name of the Giver of Life.

Benediction

Leader: Little sheep, go back into the world.

People: We go in the name of the Good Shepherd.

Leader: Little sheep, be watchful, the wolves are yet alive.

People: We go in the power of the Good Shepherd.

Leader: Little sheep, be alert, be harmless, and be wise.

People: We go because the Good Shepherd has conquered every enemy with the resurrection.

Leader: God the Creator, Christ the Redeemer, and the Holy Spirit are with us!

People: Thanks be to God! Amen.

THE FIFTH SUNDAY OF EASTER

Acts 8:26–40
Psalm 22:25–31
1 John 4:7–21
John 15:1–8

Call to Worship

Leader: The God of each new day calls us.
People: We expect an endless array of opportunities.
Leader: The God of each new beginning beckons us.
People: We anticipate new possibilities to be set before us.
Leader: The God of every fresh start awaits us.
People: We have gathered to receive anew the promises of abundant life.

Call to Confession

We love because God first loved us. Those who say they love God and hate their brothers or sisters are liars. For we cannot love God whom we have not seen, and hate those we see each day. Let us confess our sin.

Confession

Almighty God, Lover of our souls, we come to you with ruptured relationships everywhere. Breathe upon us the breath of new life. Forgive us our sin. Help us to love in deeds that reveal your presence in our life. Empower us to walk in the new life of the Christ, in whose name we pray.

Words of Assurance

God abides in everyone who dares to confess that Jesus is the Son of God. With our confession, we now abide in God's love. This is good news.

Responsive Reading

Leader: We are living testimonies!
People: May our hearts live to give praise forever.
Leader: With our redemption, our voices join with those on the other side.

People: May our hearts live to give praise forever.

Leader: From generation to generation we remember the One who preserves our lives.

People: May our hearts live to give praise forever.

Leader: We have moved from can't to can! As the most poor, by grace, we have been fed to satisfaction.

People: May our hearts live to give praise forever.

Leader: We are living testimonies. We should have been dead and erased from memory!

People: God has said that we would live on! We will continue to give God praise forever!

Offertory Invitation

Beloved, let us love one another, because love is from God. Everyone who loves is born of God and knows God. Whoever does not love does not know God, for God is love. God's love has been revealed to us through the life, death, and resurrection of God's only begotten Son. Our sacrificial giving is the only appropriate response.

Offertory Praise

God, it is by your Holy Spirit that we give. In generosity you have given unto us. Receive now our gifts to be used for others. In the name of Lavish Love, we pray.

Benediction

Leader: Jesus is the Vine.

People: God is the Vine grower.

Leader: We are the branches.

People: God is expecting fruit.

Leader: Go into the world, reaping a harvest of blessings for God

People: We will abide in God and bear much fruit.

Leader: God the Vine grower, Jesus the Vine, and the Holy Spirit, the fruit producer, are with us.

People: Thanks be to God. Amen.

THE SIXTH SUNDAY OF EASTER

Acts 10:44–48
Psalm 98
1 John 5:1–6
John 15:9–17

Call to Worship

Leader: The Living Word demands time to speak.
People: Our ears are open to hear from God.
Leader: The Mouth That Speaks Life wants to counsel with us.
People: Our spirits long to commune with God.
Leader: The Speaking God wants to impart new life this day.
People: We have come to be refreshed by the Word that never fails.

Call to Confession

The love of God is that we obey every commandment. Since we have broken the commandments, it is our time to confess.

Confession

God, the ancestors used to say that all you told them to do, they did not do. Then, they said that all you told them not to do, they did. We laughed as they confessed. We have now become them. Forgive us our sin. Help us to show you our love through the gift of the Christ, we pray.

Words of Assurance

Everyone who believes that Jesus is the Christ has been born of God, and everyone who loves the parent, loves the child. By this we know that we love the children of God, when we love God and obey God's commandments. This is our time of new beginning.

Responsive Reading

Leader: It's time to throw a party. It's time to celebrate!
People: God continues to kick tail, take names, and show out on our behalf!

Leader: Victory after victory reveals the sovereignty of our God.

People: Let's get the party going on. We owe God big-time praise.

Leader: Make a joyful noise unto the Lord.

People: We call out a great shout for the Magnificent God!

Leader: Break out the Hammonds, turn up the Leslie B-3s.

People: Tune the bass and kick it with the horn sections.

Leader: Let the elements join in as we jam.

People: The sea will roar. The hills will dance. The wind will howl. The trees will sing.

Leader: There's a party going on.

People: For the Righteous Judge is in the house!

Offertory Invitation

Who is it that conquers the world, but we who believe that Jesus Christ is the Son of God? And, this is the victory, the sharing of our faith through giving.

Offertory Praise

God, you sent One by water and blood, Jesus the Christ. The Holy Spirit has testified in us as to this truth. Receive our gifts that others may come to know. In the name of Christ we pray.

Benediction

Leader: Leave, knowing that God commands that we love one another.

People: There is no greater love than this.

Leader: God has already shown us love by sending Jesus to die for our sin.

People: Jesus has shown his love by dying and rising on our behalf.

Leader: Go now and be living witnesses to the world that Jesus lives.

People: We have been chosen and appointed.

Leader: Leave to bear good fruit! Then, whatsoever you ask in the name of Christ will be supplied.

People: We leave to love one another as God has loved us!

Leader: The God of opportunities, the Christ of possibilities, and the promised Holy Spirit are ours!

People: Hallelujah and amen!

ASCENSION SUNDAY · THE SEVENTH SUNDAY AFTER EASTER

Acts 1:1–11
Psalm 47 or Psalm 93
Ephesians 1:15–23
Luke 24:44–53

Call to Worship

Leader: Those who have fallen down this past week are welcomed to this worship.
People: We have come with our pious faces and our masks of pretense.
Leader: Those who have fallen down hard this past week are invited to this worship.
People: We have tried to fool others and ourselves about this falling down business!
Leader: Jesus went down into the grave, a victim of sinful deeds. He got up!
People: This is his day of Ascension. This means that we can get up too! Thanks be to God!

Call to Confession

Jesus has said that repentance and forgiveness of sin are to be proclaimed in his name. We have fallen! Let us confess and repent so that forgiveness is ours.

Confession

God, we have fallen and even wallowed this past week. We have fallen and felt so ashamed. We have fallen and been tempted not to make an attempt to get back up. But this day we have come to the house called by your name, for we want to get up! We want to stay up. For we want to ascend in the judgment and live with you throughout eternity. Forgive us. Pick us up. Start with us again we pray, in the name of the Christ who got up!

Words of Assurance

God put the power of getting up to work in Christ who was raised from the dead and is now seated at the right hand of God in heavenly places.

Whenever we fall down, that loving grace is available to pick us up. This is good news.

Responsive Reading

Leader: It's hand-clapping time for the Getting-Up God!
People: There will be no willy-nilly, pitty-pat clapping either!
Leader: Give it up, for the God who got up!
People: Make some noise for the One who destroyed sin, death, and hell.
Leader: Call out a shout for the Awesome God who breaks through earth and lifts above the clouds.
People: Jesus lifted off in visible sight.
Leader: That gave a new song to those who had been singing the blues!
People: Jesus overcame stormy weather and rose above every cloud.
Leader: Blessed assurance, Jesus is exalted over the earth.
People: Singing breaks out among the people of this Getting-Up God!

Offertory Invitation

Our faith in the Risen Lord calls us to show love toward all the saints. For this reason we do not cease to give thanks as we share with the world through our giving.

Offertory Praise

God, you put power to work in Christ when you raised him from the dead and seated him at your right hand in heavenly places. Today he is far above all rule, authority, power, and dominion. We give these gifts, with thanksgiving, in the Name above Every Name.

Benediction

Leader: Go! God has given you what was promised.
People: We have been clothed again with power from on high.
Leader: Go! God has blessed you indeed.
People: Jesus got up and was lifted up to the heavens with glory.
Leader: The power to be lifted above every circumstance you will face is yours.
People: We leave with songs of praise to the Ascended Christ upon our lips. Amen.

THE SEVENTH SUNDAY OF EASTER

Acts 1:15–17, 21–26
Psalm 1
1 John 5:9–13
John 17:6–19

Call to Worship

Leader: Giving honor to God this morning.
People: Have you lost it this morning?
Leader: It's testimony time. Has God been good to you this week?
People: We have gathered to give honor to God!

Call to Confession

God knows our hearts. It's time to fess up!

Confession

God, you declared that we would be happy if we did not follow the advice of the wicked or take the path of sinners. We have done exactly what you told us not to do. We find ourselves outside of your will and your way. Forgive us our sin. Put us back on the right path, we pray, in the name of the Way.

Words of Assurance

Those who believe in the Son of God have the testimony in their hearts. God has given us eternal life. Whoever has the Son has life. This is good news.

Responsive Reading

Leader: Come on and let the good times roll!
People: It is party time, for we have decided not to walk with sinners or hang out with fools.
Leader: We feast on the Word of God and meditate on precious promises both day and night.

People: We are like those beautiful trees that bloomed first in Eden. We bear good fruit and make God happy with our lives.

Leader: We have decided to kick it with God and to allow the wicked to go their way without us.

People: What we do for God prospers! The wicked will stand in judgement.

Leader: Come on and let the good times roll.

People: Throughout our days our Sovereign God watches over us and our good times will continue through eternity. The way of the wicked will ultimately perish. This is the Word of God!

Offertory Invitation

This is the testimony: God gave us eternal life and this life is in God's Son. What a privilege to partake of this good life. It's our responsibility to give so that others might know and receive Christ.

Offertory Praise

Those who believe in the Son of God have this testimony in their hearts: eternal life is ours! We offer you our thanks, Eternal One, for the greatest gift of all, the love of Christ in our hearts.

Benediction

Leader: I have made known the name of the Living Christ to you this day.

People: We have believed that God sent Jesus just for us.

Leader: I pray that as you go to make God look good in the world, you are protected by the Name above All Names.

People: The world has hated us because we do not belong. Yet we go wrapped in God's truth.

Leader: God, sanctify them in your truth for your word is truth. Now, as you have sent me, so I send them into the world as ambassadors. The Truth of God, the Love of Christ, and the Power of the Holy Spirit go with us.

People: Hallelujah and amen.

7 · Pentecost and the Following Season

The Holy Spirit arrives fresh, hot, touching, laughing, anointing, and dispatching the hidden and scared individuals into the streets. The Holy Spirit, the Comforter, sent to live in us, work on us, walk beside us to guide our daily life, comes on the scene. It's time for celebration. It's a distinct and significant occasion, for power is in the house! It's a brand new day, a brand new beginning, and a brand new season of growth, spread, and change.

"You'll receive power" is the promise of Acts 1:8. The Holy Spirit's power is necessary for the effective living of our new life in Christ. The acts and deeds of those called Christian will be noticed by all the world. The power to make a difference is ours!

Ordinary time—the long period between Pentecost and Advent—is the longest season of the Church, where we are called to live out our faith on a daily basis without any festival to celebrate. As we walk with God on a daily basis, in the mundane duties of regular existence, the worship rituals, our daily devotions, and our life of prayer will see us through.

Altar Focus

For Pentecost, red with white paraments and red balloons are needed to set the stage for fire, which not only burns and consumes, but ignites, motivates, and inspires. Red candles of assorted sizes and shapes would make a lovely addition. A banner with tongues of fire laid across the altar can assist in delivering the message of a brand new day.

The liturgical color for ordinary time is green to signify growth, which God continues to anticipate from our lives as we live without fanfare and hoopla.

PENTECOST SUNDAY

Ezekiel 37:1-14
Acts 2:1–21
Psalm 104:24–34, 35b
Romans 8:22–27
John 15:26–27, 16:4b–15

Call to Worship

Leader: People of God, I proclaim that this is the day of God's latter rain!
People: Rain, fall upon these dry and arid bones.
Leader: People of God, I decree that the still dew of refreshing will penetrate our thirsty souls.
People: Dew, descend upon our parched places.
Leader: People of God, I declare that God will breath upon us that we might fully live.
People: Breathe upon us and fill us with new and abundant life. We gather, ready to receive!
Leader: This is the day of Pentecost: the rain, the dew, and the fresh wind of God are present to minister to every need.
People: Spirit Holy, fall fresh upon us!

Call to Confession

Our lives are evidence of the dryness that overtakes and stifles creativity. Dry lives are prone to sin. God has given us the right and the ability to prophesy to the four winds that they may come and impart new life in order that we might live pleasing to God. This is our time of confession. Let us pray.

Confession

God, our bones are dried up and our hope is lost; we are cut off from you. We repent of our sin. We seek your forgiveness and grace. Rain upon us. Breath upon us. Save us from ourselves, we pray in the name of the Living Christ.

Words of Assurance

The promise from God is alive and well. "O my people, I will put my spirit within you and you shall live, and I will place you on your own soil that you might know that I, the Lord, have spoken and I will act." This is certainly good news.

Responsive Reading

Leader: Keeping it together is a difficult thing for most folks!
People: Now, that's on the real side! For we struggle to piece together our lives!
Leader: Yet on the day of Pentecost, a group of scared folks got it together.
People: And the Holy Spirit was dispatched from heaven with signs and wonders.
Leader: Suddenly there was the sound of wind and the sighting of divided tongues of fire.
People: The people were bewildered, amazed, and astonished as they were filled with fresh power.
Leader: May the glory of the Fire that is never quenched be ours forever!
People: We have received mightily from our God.
Leader: With the coming of the Holy Spirit we are renewed.
People: With the coming of the Holy Spirit we are sent forth into the world.
Leader: May the Spirit of Refreshing rejoice in the way we live our lives.
People: May our meditation always be pleasing unto God. We will bless the Sovereign One. And we will work diligently to keep it together. The power is ours. Thanks be unto God!

Offertory Invitation

The coming of the Holy Spirit indicated that the new Church had to grow up and take full responsibility for the realm of God. That mandate has reached us. Let us give generously so that the Holy Spirit may reach many others.

Offertory Praise

The Advocate has come and, God, we give you praise. The Holy Spirit testifies in our hearts of your amazing grace toward us. So, we give in order to simply say, "Thanks!" Receive our gifts in the name of Christ, we pray.

Benediction

Leader: Christ told his followers that it was to their advantage that he go away so that the Comforter might come.

People: The Spirit of Comfort goes before us into the world.

Leader: Christ told his followers that there were many things they did not fully understand.

People: The Spirit of Truth has come to speak to our hearts and to lead us in right paths.

Leader: Go into the world, enfolded in the Triune God—Creator, Redeemer, and Sustainer.

People: Hallelujah and amen.

TRINITY SUNDAY · THE FIRST SUNDAY AFTER PENTECOST

Isaiah 6:1–8
Psalm 29
Romans 8:12–17
John 3:1–17

Call to Worship

Leader: God is here! The Triune God is present with us!
People: God is revealed as the Great I Am, the Miracle Worker and the Power to Keep!
Leader: God is here! The Triune God is present to us!
People: God is revealed as the Awesome, the Absolute, and the Always Present!
Leader: God is here! The Triune God is present for us!
People: God is revealed as the God who was, the God who is, and the God who will always be!
Leader: God is here! The Triune God is present!
People: We have gathered to worship and adore the God of Yesterday, Today, and Forevermore! God is here!

Call to Confession

For all who are led by the Spirit of God are children of God. For we have not received a spirit of slavery to fall back into fear. So the fear that stagnates us grows from the sin within us! This is our time to make it right with confession. Let us pray.

Confession

Triune God, you continue to come to us and to call forth the very best from us. We fall down. We forget our destiny. We fail to heed your call. Forgive our sin. Restore us with your Spirit of Adoption. We pray in the name of the Only Begotten Son.

Words of Assurance

Now that the Holy Spirit has touched our lips with confession, our guilt has departed and our sin is blotted out. This opens the way for us to respond to God's call: "Who will go for us?" We can now willingly say, "Here I am, Lord, send me!"

Responsive Reading

Leader: Give it up for the Creating God who has shown glory and strength!
People: We give God the glory and worship due. Rap is not needed, simply words of thanks.
Leader: Give it up for the Word made flesh!
People: We give Jesus Christ the glory and worship due. Death could not kill him. Resurrection is ours due to him. All praise to God's Son.
Leader: Give it up for the Power and the Glory!
People: We give the Holy Spirit praise for the ability to make something beautiful out of our lives!
Leader: The Triune God is powerful, full of majesty, and inspiring awe throughout the world.
People: We have tried to rhyme our wonder; we have made feeble attempts to create poems and even songs of praise. Yet when we consider God's splendor, we are speechless mortals who can only say "Wow! What an Awesome God!"

Offertory Invitation

Just as Moses lifted up the serpent in the wilderness, so must God's Son be lifted up, that whosoever believes in him may have eternal life. For God so loved the world until giving became fashionable! Now, it's our turn to share in God's generous plan.

Offertory Praise

The wind blows where it chooses and we hear the sound, But, God, only you know where it comes from or where it goes. Thank you for sending the powerful winds of the Holy Spirit upon our lives so that giving has become our loving response. Receive these gifts in the name of your Conquering Son, we pray.

Benediction

Leader: The Triune God sits enthroned forever. Now, may the Eternal One grant us strength and bless us all with great Shalom!
People: Hallelujah to the Trinity. Amen.

PROPER 4 · SUNDAY BETWEEN MAY 29 AND JUNE 4

1 Samuel 3:1–10, (11–20)
Psalm 139:1–6, 13–18
2 Corinthians 4:5–12
Mark 2:23–3:6

Call to Worship

Leader: What are you doing here this morning?
People: We have heard a clarion call to worship.
Leader: For what have you come this morning?
People: We want to see God more clearly.
Leader: The Word of God is present.
People: Speak, God; we your people need to hear a fresh word from you!
Leader: Are you prepared to listen?
People: Speak, God, for your servants are listening!

Call to Confession

Hidden sin brings down the certain wrath of God. Eli was told by God, "I am going to punish your house forever because of your hidden sin." The time of honest confession is at hand. Let us ask for forgiveness of all that separates us from God and prevents us from hearing God's Word. Shall we pray?

Confession

"Here I am, Lord," I have been discovered. I am a sinner in need of your grace. "Here I am, Lord," your Word has uncovered my sin. Do not hide your face from me. "Here I am, Lord," in need of your mercy. Forgive me. Restore me. Make me whole, I pray, in the name of Christ.

Words of Assurance

It was God who said, "Let light shine out of darkness." This same God has shone in our hearts to give us the knowledge of glory in the face of Jesus Christ. We have called. God has answered. This is good news.

Responsive Reading

Leader: Hey, God, it's us again. You already know who we are!

People: You are so well acquainted with all that we do! We cannot slip and slide with you. You are everywhere!

Leader: You have gone before us and when we get there we meet you.

People: You remain behind us and peep all our deeds done in the dark!

Leader: We can't even get a lie past you! You know our thoughts before they hit our lips!

People: There's no need to ask "What's up with you?" You are too tough to be fooled or connived!

Leader: God, you are the bomb! You are so bad that words cannot describe you!

People: You knew us before our conception. Before we were thoughts in our parents' minds, you had already designed our life and crafted our future with you.

Leader: We praise you! For we recognize that we are made in your image! We are wonderful. And that's a "lite" word to use!

People: We have an intimate connection, God. It really is all about you and me!

Leader: Since you saw me before I was formed, there is no need for me to play a part for you!

People: How awesome are the thoughts you think of us, O God. How great to realize that you always have our best in mind.

Leader: Try counting the good thoughts God has for you!

People: We are not equipped to count the number of sand grains laying on every beach! And God's thoughts of us are more numerous than all these combined! Suffice it to say, that we and God are tight! That's good enough to know!

Offertory Invitation

While we live, we are always being given up to some form of death for the sake of Jesus Christ. We do this in order that Jesus may be made visible in our mortal flesh. With our giving, others may come to see Jesus and be saved. Let us freely share.

Offertory Praise

The Sabbath was made for humankind, and not humankind for the Sabbath. So as we have received this day of rest and re-creation, we offer to you the fruit of our hands in thanks. May the Living Christ be honored with our gifts, we pray.

Benediction

Leader: Friends, we leave knowing that we have this treasure in earthen vessels!

People: It is clear that the extraordinary power within us and at work on our behalf belongs to God.

Leader: We have nothing on our own, but with God on our side we leave assured.

People: We are afflicted in every way, but not crushed. We are perplexed, but not driven to despair. We are persecuted, but not forsaken. We are struck down, but we are not destroyed. For the life of Jesus Christ is at work in us, on us, and through us.

Leader: Thanks be to God for the victory! Go to be the Church, alive in the world.

People: Hallelujah and amen.

PROPER 5 · SUNDAY BETWEEN JUNE 5 AND JUNE 11

1 Samuel 8:4-11 (12-15), 16-20
Psalm 138
2 Corinthians 4:13–5:1
Mark 3:20–35

Call to Worship

Leader: Rebellion is in the air!
People: But we have gathered to give God praise!
Leader: Hard hearts have discovered lesser gods.
People: But we have gathered to give God glory!
Leader: The spirit of rejection has set up camp.
People: But we have gathered to give God honor.
Leader: The time of choice has arrived.
People: We have gathered to worship the Ancient of Days!

Call to Confession

God knows that we have blown it again! Another week and another series of turning away from God. It is written, "From the day I brought them out of Egypt to this day, they have forsaken me and are serving other gods. Solemnly warn them, and show them the ways of the King." Our cover has been blown too. It's time to confess our sin.

Confession

God, we have come to offer the sacrifice of praise. And, we have come with sin in our lives. Forgive us. Restore us. We want to offer earnest and honest worship to your name. We pray in the name of the Redeemer of All.

Words of Assurance

With confession, we do not lose heart. For though our outer nature is wasting away, our inner nature is being renewed day by day. This is good news.

Responsive Reading

Leader: God's in the house!
People: We offer sincere praise.
Leader: God's on the scene!
People: We fall in humble adoration for the benefits we have received.
Leader: God's steadfast love and faithfulness are on exhibit.
People: The exalted name of God is righteous. The Word of God stands alone.
Leader: God calls. We respond. We ask for strength. God responds.
People: Word up, God is due big-time praise.
Leader: It's time to make merry music.
People: We bring out our best songs for the glory of God.
Leader: Great is the Omnipotent One who sits high and looks low.
People: Mighty is our God who condescends in order to lift us up!
Leader: We walk in the midst of trouble.
People: God's right hand protects us. We are delivered from every evil.
Leader: God's purpose will be fulfilled.
People: We are on purpose for God. For we are the divine work of God's powerful hand.

Offertory Invitation

For we know that if the earthly house we live in is destroyed, we have a building from God, a house not made with hands, eternal in the heavens. Our sharing allows others the opportunity to know and to share.

Offertory Praise

God, as everything is for your sake, please accept our gifts, so that your grace may extend to more and more people throughout the world. Our thanksgiving continually increases due to the glory of the name and work of your matchless Son, Jesus Christ.

Benediction

Leader: Go home to the world. Remember they are in need of your care.
People: We leave to find our wayward family.
Leader: Remember that whoever does the will of God is your sister, brother, mother, and father.
People: There are no orphans! We are the family of God.
Leader: Go home to the world! Remember they are in need of your care.
People: Hallelujah and amen.

PROPER 6 · SUNDAY BETWEEN JUNE 12 AND JUNE 18

1 Samuel 15:34–16:13
Psalm 20
2 Corinthians 5:6–17
Mark 4:26–34

Call to Worship

Leader: The God of tiny seedlings calls us.
People: We have heard God's call through the new blooms of flowers.
Leader: The God of tiny sparrows summons us.
People: We have heard God's call through the melodious songs of the chirping birds.
Leader: The God of sunshine and new harvest demands an audience.
People: We gather to give praise and thanks to the God of New Seasons and New Times!

Call to Confession

When we gather, God demands, "Sanctify yourselves and then come to me." It is time to confess our sin.

Confession

God of tiny things, you know the issues of sin that lie tucked away within my heart. They are the little things I want to overlook, not pay attention to, and neglect to correct. Yet, as the God of the tiny creatures, you see, notice, and mark my sin. Forgive me. Restore me. Let the light of your righteousness shine into every corner of my heart. For it's in the name of the Light of Glory that I pray.

Words of Assurance

God does not see as mortals see. For we look at the outward appearance. God looks at our hearts. Hearts cleansed by confession honor God. This is good news!

Responsive Reading

Leader: Before we call, God answers!

People: Before we fall, God responds!

Leader: The name of God is our strong protection.

People: We have help from God's sanctuary and support that cannot be seen.

Leader: God remembers the sacrifices of our lives.

People: God longs to fulfill our hearts' desires and provide us with loving favor.

Leader: We can give out a shout for victory, in the midst of the storms.

People: We can wave the banners of triumph even while the war rages around us.

Leader: We are God's anointed.

People: We are God's appointed.

Leader: We are supported by the strong right hand of God.

People: There is only one place to be and that is on the right side of the Almighty.

Leader: Some take security in war weapons, others seek to build monetary treasures on earth.

People: But, our stake is in the Ancient of Days. That's more than enough!

Leader: Many will fall at our side; it will seem as if destruction is overwhelming.

People: Yet we will stand in the strength of the Almighty, who answers before we call.

Offertory Invitation

We walk by faith and not by sight! Our giving results in outcomes we cannot see. Yet, it is because of our faith that we will generously share our gifts.

Offertory Praise

God, each of us must appear before the judgment seat of Christ, so that we may receive recompense for what has been done in our body, whether good or evil. Receive now the works of our hands that it might be on

record that we willingly return thanks for all you have given us.
In the name of Matchless Love, we pray.

Benediction

Leader: Go into the world, knowing the reverence of God.
People: We leave to try and persuade others by our lives.
Leader: Go into the world, boasting of the mighty deeds of God.
People: We leave to give our God praise by the activities we will engage in during the week.
Leader: Go into the world, knowing that the old has passed away.
People: We leave remembering that the old has passed away. We are new creations in Jesus Christ.
Leader: The blessings of the Ancient of Days, the love of the Redeemer of Souls, and the keeping power of the Holy Spirit will make every day a new beginning.
People: Hallelujah and amen!

PROPER 7 · JUNETEENTH OBSERVANCE
SUNDAY BETWEEN JUNE 19 AND JUNE 25
1 Samuel 17:1–23, 32-49
Psalm 9:9–20
2 Corinthians 6:1–13
Mark 4:35–41

Call to Worship

Leader: Goliath is on the way!
People: We come in the strong name of the Sovereign God.
Leader: Goliath is big and has great weapons of war.
People: We come in the strong name of the Sovereign God.
Leader: Goliath breaths out much smack, filled with threats.
People: We come in the strong name of the Sovereign God.
Leader: Goliath doesn't simply talk; many have fallen at his side.
People: Goliath is only temporary. We come in the strong name of the Eternal God. Every Goliath will die. For on 19 June 1865, the Goliath of slavery died in every southern state. Juneteenth was born! Our God reigns over every Goliath! Thanks be unto the Almighty!

Call to Confession

God has declared, "At an acceptable time I have listened to you, and on the day of salvation I have helped you. See, now is the acceptable time. Now is the day of salvation." Let's confess the sin that keeps us from being acceptable unto God.

Confession

God, we have been terrified of Goliath! We have stopped and paid homage to the strength, the size, and the language of a mere human god. We have sinned. Forgive us. Help us to move past every Goliath with our eyes focused on you. Only you are a source of salvation and wholeness. We pray in the name of Jesus Christ.

Words of Assurance

Now that we have confessed our sin, we are servants of the Most High God! And as servants of God we have been granted the power of God with weapons of righteousness for the right hand and for the left. We are alive! This is good news.

Responsive Reading

Leader: God is our sure defense!
People: We have been deceived into believing that hidden money, suburban homes, big cars, and lots of "bling, bling" would make us secure.
Leader: God is our sure defense!
People: We have a habit of forgetting who birthed us, brought us safely across the Middle Passage, and keeps us day by day in this foreign land.
Leader: God is our sure defense!
People: In good times we sing of God's past faithfulness and remember the stories of the ancestors. But when Goliath shows up, we have a tendency to lean towards our street sense!
Leader: God is our sure defense!
People: See what we suffer from those who hate us. Remember our afflictions down through the years.
Leader: God is our sure defense!
People: It would help to see a little blood shed, some retaliation for all the wrongs we have suffered.
Leader: God is our sure defense!
People: This nation seems to sink lower and lower with regards to morals and ethics. There is hesitation to even talk of reparations for all our years of free toil.
Leader: God is our sure defense!
People: God executes justice. The wicked are snared in the work of their own hands.
Leader: God is our sure defense!
People: We have never been forgotten and our hope is not dead! For every need has been met. We serve the God who specializes in making ways out of no ways! We remember Juneteenth.
Leader: God is our sure defense!
People: Rise up, O Sovereign God! Do not allow heathens to prevail. Put fear into the heart of every Goliath. For you are the only sure defense!

Offertory Invitation

As we work together with Christ, our sharing urges others to accept the grace we have found in God. Let's be generous in our giving.

Offertory Praise

God, we have spoken earnestly with our gifts. Our hearts are open wide to you. There is no restriction in our affections. Accept now the works of our labors, we pray in the name of Goliath's Ultimate Destroyer!

Benediction

Leader: Peace, be still! This is the command to everything that you will face this week.
People: The winds of life will batter us, and the waves of daily living will rush in upon us.
Leader: Peace, be still! Why are you afraid? Have you no faith? Jesus has already spoken!
People: The winds and the waves obey his voice. We leave to do the same.
Leader: The calming presence of God, the sure defense of Christ, and the enabling power of the Holy Spirit be your shalom!
People: Hallelujah and amen!

PROPER 8 · SUNDAY BETWEEN JUNE 26 AND JULY 2

2 Samuel 1:1, 17–27
Psalm 130
2 Corinthians 8:7–15
Mark 5:21–43

Call to Worship

Leader: This is the day to reach out and touch.
People: The loving touch of Christ has drawn us here.
Leader: This is the day to reach out and be touched.
People: The healing power of Christ has brought us here.
Leader: This is the day to reach out with loving touch to the community.
People: The connecting touch of Christ ministers throughout the world.
Leader: This is the day. This is the place. The touch of the Divine is ours.
People: We give thanks for a sensitive Savior!

Call to Confession

How the mighty have fallen during the week gone by! We left last week with great intentions to live our best for God. The struggles of the week have challenged, tested, and beat many of us down. With all of our good hopes, the mighty have fallen. It's time to confess and start again.

Confession

Gracious and loving God, you love us better than we love ourselves. Like David we can say that your love is wonderful, surpassing the human love we know. Yet, we have fallen snare to the weapons of the enemy of our souls. Forgive us our sin. Restore us to a love relationship with you, we pray in the name of the Christ.

Words of Assurance

Jesus Christ hastens to those with repentant hearts of confession. He assures us, "Child of mine, your faith has made you whole. Go and be whole." This is good news.

Responsive Reading

Leader: God, it seems as if the bottom has fallen out of the jar that held our dreams and hopes.

People: Life is a mess! Chaos is everywhere! There is no spot where confusion is not!

Leader: God, we need your immediate attention! Please listen up!

People: We are facing difficult times. There seems to be little love for us anywhere.

Leader: We know that you keep record of the wrongs done. Can't you number the many times we have been pushed aside, held down, and kept down?

People: We know that you are a forgiving God. The whole world counts on your tender mercy.

Leader: It's a good thing that you are a forgiving God who blots out sin. For we would not be able to stand in your presence. We appreciate that loving kindness is your nature.

People: God, hear our prayers. Our souls yearn for your restoration. We need to know that you care.

Leader: We are waiting to hear from you.

People: We are longing to know that you hear us.

Leader: We seek a new day, with new beginnings and fresh hope.

People: We look for a time when it will be our turn to be first and special.

Leader: You have a reputation for coming to see about the oppressed.

People: And when you have arrived, love, power, and redemption come with you. Even so, come soon with deliverance, Good God!

Offertory Invitation

Now as we excel in everything, in faith, in speech, in knowledge, in utmost eagerness, and in our love for Jesus Christ, so we want to excel in our generous giving unto a gracious God.

Offertory Praise

Jesus Christ, our Redeemer, though you were rich, yet for our sakes you became poor, so that by your poverty we might become rich. We are rich in your loving kindness. Receive our offerings, given in your name, we pray.

Benediction

Leader: Go! Be on the alert for those holy interruptions in your life.
People: Jesus specialized in being interrupted and doing ministry on the spot.
Leader: Go! Be ready to offer help, aid, and assistance to those who interrupt your days.
People: Jesus reached out and touched with compassion those who were in need.
Leader: Go, in the creative energy of God, the ready compassion of Christ, and the enriching touch of the Holy Spirit. The power to touch is yours!
People: Hallelujah and amen!

PROPER 9 · SUNDAY BETWEEN JULY 3 AND JULY 9

2 Samuel 5:1–5, 9-10
Psalm 48
2 Corinthians 12:2–10
Mark 6:1–13

Call to Worship

Leader: The God of challenge and possibilities calls us to gather.
People: We come to be refreshed, renewed, and revived.
Leader: The God of all tribes summons us to greater service.
People: We come to give honor and praise to the Ruler of Nations.

Call to Confession

God has called us to higher heights than we can even imagine. We have failed to live up to our potential. It's confession time.

Confession

God of David, the little shepherd boy, we too have been summoned from the backgrounds and anointed for your service. We have neglected to do all that we can. We have done things unpleasing in your sight. Forgive us our sin. Use us in your service. We pray in the name of the Good Shepherd.

Words of Assurance

David became greater and greater, for the God of hosts was with him. That same God is with us. This is good news!

Responsive Reading

Leader: We don't own too much in our own communities.
People: "They" come in and buy up all the stores.
Leader: Tax breaks and zoning ordinances allow others to buy up our neighborhoods.
People: "They" sell the gas. "They" sell spoiled foods. "They" even sell our hair products!

Leader: We don't own very much in our own communities.

People: But, the House of The Living God is ours! "They" don't own this place of refuge!

Leader: We have a safe space. We have a hiding place. We have sanctuary.

People: "They" can't touch this! We have sacrificed to ensure that the name of our God reigns here.

Leader: In this place we remember God's love in action towards us.

People: In this place we recall God's miracle working power on our behalf.

Leader: This sacred spot is encircled by God's army of angels.

People: What a firm foundation has been secured for us and our posterity.

Leader: Goodness and Mercy are in this place.

People: Hallelujahs and loud praises issue forth in this place.

Leader: The next generation will know our love for God.

People: The next generation will continue to know God's everlasting love for us.

Offertory Invitation

It's boasting time! We have been so tremendously blessed. Now, it's our time to boast in our Lavishly Generous God through our sacrificial giving, which will benefit others.

Offertory Praise

God, we present a token of our health and wealth to you in the form of offerings. You have promised us that your grace is sufficient for us and that your power is made perfect in weakness. We pray that these gifts will be so multiplied that the world might come to know you. We pray in the name of the one in whom we boast, Jesus Christ.

Benediction

Leader: God has called us together and spoken to our hearts. Leave to be the Church!

People: God has equipped us and now sends us out into the world with authority over the unclean spirits.

Leader: Go into the world and bid them God's shalom.

People: We leave to proclaim him as Sovereign in our lives.

Leader: God the Healer, Christ the Savior, and the Anointing of the Holy Spirit go with us!

People: Hallelujah and amen.

PROPER 10 · SUNDAY BETWEEN JULY 10 AND JULY 16

2 Samuel 6:1–5, 12b–19
Psalm 24
Ephesians 1:3–14
Mark 6:14-29

Call to Worship

Leader: From the ravages of the past week, God calls.
People: From the wrecks we have made with our lives, we respond.
Leader: God longs to tabernacle among us.
People: Our yearning hearts say, even so, come Christ Jesus.

Call to Confession

The tender mercies of God are new every morning. Great is God's faithfulness to all who will turn from their wicked ways and seek God's face with confession. This is our time. This is the place of repentance.

Confession

God, sin keeps us from the abundance you have created for us. We long to be in communion with you. We seek to be your agents in the world. Yet, we fall down in sin. Forgive us. Restore us. Pick us up and cleanse us with the water of your living Word. We pray in the name of Amazing Grace.

Words of Assurance

Blessed be the God of our Lord Jesus Christ, who has blessed us in Christ with every spiritual blessing. In Christ we have redemption through his blood, the forgiveness of our sin, according to the riches of his grace that have been lavished upon us. Indeed, this is good news!

Responsive Reading

Leader: Say the name, say the name!
People: The Creator of all the world is God.

Leader: Say the name, say the name!

People: The world, God owns it. The seas, God made them. The hills, give it up for God!

Leader: There is none greater. There are none more masterful. There are none equal to the Almighty God!

People: Only those who are living right can come before God.

Leader: God will only deal with those whose motives are pure and whose intentions are honorable.

People: These are the kind who can depend on God to always be there.

Leader: God seekers and God pleasers can demand an audience with the Truth of the Ages.

People: When we live right we receive every blessing from God.

Leader: So lift up your hands. Give out a shout! Make way for God!

People: God is the Captain in charge! God reigns over all! It is our privilege to say God's righteous name!

Offertory Invitation

With all wisdom and insight we have been shown the mystery of God's will, according to the gift we have received in Jesus Christ. In him, since we first believed, we have been marked with the promised Holy Spirit, who calls us to share with the world.

Offertory Praise

God, we thank you for adopting us as your children through Jesus Christ, according to the good pleasure of your loving will. Please accept these, our gifts, as we offer them in his holy and righteous name.

Benediction

Leader: Go into the world and testify to the glory of God through Jesus Christ.

People: We go, remembering that John the Baptist lost his head for proclaiming this sacred name.

Leader: Go into the world and testify to the glory of God through Jesus Christ.

People: We go, mindful of the fact that John died in faith, to live again.

Leader: The God of Creation, the Christ of Resurrection, and the Holy Spirit work on our behalf!

People: Hallelujah and amen.

PROPER 11 · SUNDAY BETWEEN JULY 17 AND JULY 23

2 Samuel 7:1–14a
Psalm 89:20–37
Ephesians 2:11–22
Mark 6:30–34, 53–56

Call to Worship

Leader: The Enabling God calls us to worship.
People: All week we have made attempts to worship, but we are a rebellious people.
Leader: The Lover of our Souls invites every rebellious spirit to be subject this morning.
People: We love God, who hears our cries. We submit, with reverence, to a time of worship.

Call to Confession

God wants to commune with us and knows every excuse we would offer that hinders this. Our resolve fails. We do the things we hate. We don't do the things we desire. So, we find ourselves in need of a period of confession. Let us pray.

Confession

God, we continue to wrestle with our weaknesses. We find ourselves struggling, yet yielding to sin. Forgive us. Strengthen us by your power. Raise us up to new life, we pray in the name of the Christ.

Words of Assurance

In Jesus Christ, those of us who were far off have been brought near to God by the blood of the New Covenant. For Jesus is our peace. This is good news.

Responsive Reading

Leader: David was called and anointed by God, preparing the way for God's earthly sojourn.

People: David was found faithful in his love for God.

Leader: God established his family linage and promised him good success.

People: We are the heirs of that covenant promise. God is our redeemer and the Rock of our salvation.

Leader: God's strong hand was upon David's house. We are the Davidic offspring, a strong succession of royal servants of the Most High.

People: We refuse to walk away from God's Law. We will follow God's commands.

Leader: There are serious consequences for turning away from God.

People: God's loving kindness keeps us striving to live holy and faithful.

Leader: God's Word is established forever. God does not lie!

People: The sovereign throne of God reigns supreme.

Leader: The promises of God are more secure than the tides of the moon.

People: The promises of God are as enduring as the heaven's sky.

Offertory Invitation

Remember that we have not always been the royal heirs of the promise! We have been blessed with adoption. Now we are no longer strangers and aliens of the Covenant, but citizens with the saints and members of the household of God. To encourage others to share this heritage, let's be generous in our giving.

Offertory Praise

God, we know what it feels like to be the "outsider"! We have experienced this position and didn't like it at all. We give so that no others will have to remain outside. Accept our offerings in the name of the Holy One who includes us all, we pray.

Benediction

Leader: Nathan bids us "Go into the world, do all you have in mind, for God is with us."

People: We leave as those who have been called and taught by Christ due to his loving compassion.

Leader: Go into the world, growing into holy temples in Christ.

People: We leave as those called by God, redeemed by Christ's blood, and encouraged by the gift of the Holy Spirit. For this we are truly thankful. Hallelujah and amen.

PROPER 12 · SUNDAY BETWEEN JULY 24 AND JULY 30

2 Samuel 11:1–15
Psalm 14
Ephesians 3:14–21
John 6:1–21

Call to Worship

Leader: This is the station where we gather the fishes and the loaves.
People: We have come hungry for bread that satisfies.
Leader: This is the filling station where we receive oil for our lamps.
People: We have come thirsty for water that is eternal.
Leader: The Bread of Life and the Living Water are here.
People: We come to worship in spirit and in truth.

Call to Confession

The nation was at war. David was both head of the State as well as the Church. David was at the wrong place, at the wrong time. David fell into sin, raping another man's wife. He was known as the man after God's own heart. Yet he was caught in sin. Nathan the prophet came to call him to repent. This is the time for our honest confession.

Confession

God we are no different than David. We have done wrong. We have sinned. We have fallen from your grace. Like David we ask that you wash us from our sin. Restore us with your Holy Spirit. Live in us, we pray.

Words of Assurance

The Living God seeks those who come in repentance. With confession our sin is removed. We have a right to an audience with the Divine. This is good news.

Responsive Reading

Leader: Only a fool would doubt that there is a living God!
People: There are those who are not real bright. They do awful deeds. They live immoral lives. And they think that God is not aware or does not care about their evil.

Leader: Can't you see God looking over the bannisters of heaven seeking those who dare to do the right thing?
People: It seems as if the world has gone mad. And that stupidity has not bypassed our community! We have a generation that tends to behave like heathens! Violence and swearing is their style.
Leader: We have a responsibility to take the Living God to the streets! We cannot sit by and watch a nation forget God!
People: Thank God for gospel rappers, Christian hip-hoppers, and street evangelists who are constantly seeking methods of interpreting our God to the "now" generation!
Leader: There are many contrary plans to cause us to forsake the God of the ancestors.
People: We will not fall prey to foolishness. God has a firm history with us.
Leader: Our hopes are anchored in the Ancient of Days.
People: Our dreams of deliverance for Zion will come to pass!

Offertory Invitation

Jesus fed over five thousand with a little boy's lunch. When everyone had eaten, the disciples gathered up leftovers. It happened because one brave young man dared to risk sharing the little that he had. It's our turn to share so that the increase may continue.

Offertory Praise

Indeed the prophet who was to come into the world has taught us the miracle of sharing. Gracious God, we give in his honor and in his name. Receive these our fish and loaves, we pray.

Benediction

Leader: I pray that according to the riches of God's glory you may be granted strength in your inner being with the power of the Holy Spirit, and that Christ may dwell in your hearts through faith.
People: We are rooted and grounded in love. And we pray that you may have the power to comprehend, with all the saints, what is the breadth and length and height and depth and to know the love of Christ that surpasses knowledge, so that you may be filled with all the fullness of God.
Leader: Now unto God, who by the power at work within us is able to accomplish abundantly far more than all we can ask or imagine, to this God be glory in the Church and in Christ Jesus to all generations, forever and forever.
People: It is so. Amen!

PROPER 13 · SUNDAY BETWEEN JULY 31 AND AUGUST 6

2 Samuel 11:26–12:13a
Psalm 51:1–12
Ephesians 4:1–16
John 6:24–35

Call to Worship

Leader: The God who hears lamentations waits on us.
People: We gather, leaving many laments in the night.
Leader: The God who knows heavy hearts waits on us.
People: We come, bringing the pain that our smiles try to hide.
Leader: The God who understands grieved spirits waits on us.
People: We come, bringing our brokenness as well as our joy.
Leader: Come with every imaginable feeling. God is already at work on our behalf.
People: Thanks be unto God!

Call to Confession

We live in a constant state of confusion, fear, apprehension, and uncertainty. When our lives are in a state of flux, we are more prone to move away from God and to sin. This is our time for confession.

Confession

Mighty Deliverer, as your children, we come in contrition. We have sinned and done evil in your sight. Like David, we would like to believe that we will never abuse our power, our position, or our privilege. But, like David, we have done those things we purposed never to do. Forgive us. Restore us to right relationship with you, we pray, in the name of Christ.

Words of Assurance

The grace of God covers our sin. The blood of Christ blots out our sin. The power of the Holy Spirit cancels the dominion of sin in us. This is mighty good news.

Responsive Reading

Leader: Mercy! Mercy! Mercy! Sometimes this is all we can pray!
People: God's steadfast love is willing to look beyond our faults and help us when we are in need.
Leader: Tide, Cheer, nor Oxodol can wipe out the mess we have made with our lives!
People: Nothing but the blood of Jesus Christ can wash us clean.
Leader: Our personal knowledge of sin is overwhelming. Even when others don't know, God does!
People: Every sin is "personal" with God! Regardless of whom we intend to wrong, it hurts God!
Leader: It is a wonder that God has not wiped us all off the face of the earth.
People: God would be blameless, for we mess up, big time.
Leader: God seeks truth. We perpetuate lies.
People: We are guilty as charged.
Leader: God, take this bent toward sin away!
People: God, help us to stand up straight and look into your face with honest hearts.
Leader: Give us new hearts, Dear God.
People: Put a new and a right spirit within us.
Leader: Please don't take your Holy Spirit away from us.
People: Give us back our joy and allow songs of praise to sustain us in the days to come.

Offertory Invitation

There is one body and one Spirit, just as we are called to one hope, in Jesus Christ. Our giving allows others to heed this same call. Let's be generous as we share.

Offertory Praise

God, in the midst of plenty there is yet so much lack. Please receive our gifts in hopes that they provide nourishment to minds, bodies, souls, and spirits. For we give in the name of the Supreme Giver.

Benediction

Leader: Go and share the Living Bread.
People: The world is hungry for the Bread that gives life.

Leader: Whoever comes to Christ will never be hungry.
People: Whoever believes in Christ will never be thirsty.
Leader: Go, being bread and water in the world that you will touch. God the Creator, God, the Son, and God the Holy Spirit give you the power!
People: Hallelujah and amen.

PROPER 14 · SUNDAY BETWEEN AUGUST 7 AND AUGUST 13

2 Samuel 18:5–9, 15, 31–33
Psalm 130
Ephesians 4:25–5:2
John 6:35, 41–51

Call to Worship

Leader: The God who created and loves families summons us.
People: We bring the joy of our family with us this day.
Leader: The God who knows the painful situations of families calls us.
People: We come with the hurts of broken relationships in our families.
Leader: The God who can heal and restore bonds of love is here.
People: We come with our need for wholeness and family ties.
Leader: In our worship, the God of restoration will move to enable our every need.
People: We come to offer praise unto the Most High.

Call to Confession

God calls us to put away false masks of pretense and to speak the truth to our neighbors, for we are members of the same family. There is no family present without its share of broken relationships. This is our time to confess both our need and our sin.

Confession

Great Sustainer, we come this day with humble hearts seeking your divine intervention within our families. For like the families represented in holy scriptures, ours are just as messed up. We are part of the problem. We cannot divorce ourselves from the situations. We ask your forgiveness for the sin in our lives. We need your restoration so that we might be part of the healing solution. We come with hope. We come in the name of Christ, who fostered family and community by his life.

Words of Assurance

Let no evil talk come out of your mouth. Only use those words that will be useful for the building up of each person you encounter so that you are a giver of grace to those who hear you. Be an imitator of God, as beloved children, and live in the power of Christ's love for you. God loves and accepts us. This is good news.

Responsive Reading

Leader: Make noise in this house for El Shaddai.
People: We give out a shout of praise in every place for the wonders of the God who provides more than enough.
Leader: We serve a mighty God.
People: History recalls the wonders of God throughout our life.
Leader: For our journey with God did not start in a state of slavery.
People: We are the original works of the Almighty. Africa is the home of humankind!
Leader: And since the Creation of those of dust, God has been more than good.
People: God made covenant to be more than enough.
Leader: God has kept this promise and never failed.
People: God promised to send salvation and deliverance.
Leader: God so loved us until the promise was kept in person!
People: We serve an awesome God.
Leader: It makes good sense to give honor and reverence to a Worthy God.
People: Our mamas didn't raise no fools! We will praise the Ancient of Days forever!

Offertory Invitation

We are admonished to be careful with how we live, not being unwise, but making the most of our time, for the days in which we live are so filled with evil. We are not to be foolish, but understanding of what is the will of God. And we know that God desires the world to be saved. Our giving enables God's will.

Offertory Praise

God, like Solomon we ask that you give your generous servants understanding minds to win others, being able to discern between what is good and evil. For only you govern the nations. Therefore, we pray that you receive these, our gifts, to be used to your greater service, in the name of the Christ.

Benediction

Leader: Leave, walking in the ways of God, keeping the holy commandments in your hearts.
People: We leave to walk this way before our families, knowing that this honors God and lengthens life.
Leader: Leave, singing psalms and hymns and spiritual songs among yourselves.
People: We leave to give praise and make melody to the Sovereign God, especially within our homes.
Leader: Leave, giving thanks unto God at all times and for everything in the name of Jesus Christ.
People: We leave filled with fresh hope and the power of the Holy Spirit.
Leader: And the world will know that you are Christians by your love. God the Creator, God the Son, and God the Holy Spirit make it possible.
People: Hallelujah and amen.

PROPER 15 · SUNDAY BETWEEN AUGUST 14 AND AUGUST 20

1 Kings 2:10–12, 3:3–14
Psalm 111
Ephesians 5:15–20
John 6:51–58

Call to Worship

Leader: The Wisdom of the Ages is present to give counsel.
People: We come with our issues and concerns.
Leader: The Way Maker yearns to point us in new directions.
People: We come with our confusion and perplexities.
Leader: The Giver of Every Good Gift longs to bless us.
People: We have come to worship and offer praise.

Call to Confession

Solomon asked God for an understanding mind to discern between good
and evil. It is obvious that this is the mind that we need, for our behaviors
have not been pleasing to God. This is our time to confess.

Confession

God, you asked Solomon what he wanted. We are yet searching to discover what satisfies us. Of course, we have chosen the wrong things. We
have followed our own ways. We have sinned. Forgive us, we pray, in the
name of the One Born to Die.

Words of Assurance

The Bright and Morning Star is great in steadfast love, faithful in righteousness, and constant in forgiving our sin. This is our good news!

Responsive Reading

Leader: Call out the highest praise!
People: Hallelujah in the highest!
Leader: Give up your thanksgiving!

People: Thanks unto the Almighty!

Leader: The works of God can be studied but never duplicated!

People: Honor, majesty, and righteousness stand alone.

Leader: Integrity is the watchword of the Ancient of Days.

People: Grace and mercy are offered to us daily.

Leader: We have heard the testimonies of miracles in days gone by.

People: The Covenant Maker provides miracles in our midst.

Leader: Love is present in abundance.

People: The Bread of Life sustains us.

Leader: Water that Satisfies springs up in dry places.

People: "Power to the people" is the slogan of the Generous One.

Leader: From everlasting to everlasting the Word of Life is established.

People: Awesome God! Awesome God! Totally awesome is our God! Knowing this is the beginning of wisdom. Keeping a right relationship is our purpose. We offer the highest praise! Hallelujah!

Offertory Invitation

Be careful, then, how you live, not as unwise people but as wise. Know that you can't beat God in giving. For your giving more opens the way to receiving more.

Offertory Praise

Spirit of the Living God, we sing psalms and hymns and spiritual songs among ourselves, singing and making melody in our hearts unto you. And with our giving we participate in being your blessing extended around the world. For this opportunity we give thanks, in the name of Jesus Christ.

Benediction

Leader: It's time to go and eat!

People: We leave to feast from the Bread of Life.

Leader: Whoever eats of this Bread will live forever.

People: We will pass the Bread wherever we go!

Leader: The Bread Giver, the Bread of Life, and the Bread Preserver go before us. It's time to go and eat!

People: Hallelujah and amen!

PROPER 16 · SUNDAY BETWEEN AUGUST 21 AND AUGUST 27

1 Kings 8:1, 6, 10–11, 22–30
Psalm 84
Ephesians 6:10–20
John 6:56–69

Call to Worship

Leader: The Cloud of Glory fills this house!
People: We are the ark of God's holy covenant.
Leader: The angels and cherubim give God praise!
People: The Spirit of God fills our mouth with loud "Hosannas" as we enter this time of worship.

Call to Confession

There is none like the Keeper of Israel who keeps covenant with us. We are the ones who fail to keep and preserve the covenant we made with God. In this sacred time, let us offer confession for our sin.

Confession

Sovereign God, heed the cry and prayer of your servants today. Let your eyes be open day and night toward the sanctuary we are for you. Cleanse the sin of our hearts. Let your Word wash our spirits. Forgive us as we pray in the name of Abundant Truth.

Words of Assurance

God has guaranteed that, "My name shall be there, that your prayers may be heard." Forgiveness and restoration belong to us. This is good news.

Responsive Reading

Leader: The More than Marvelous One inhabits this dwelling place.
People: What a joy to be in the presence of the One who commands songs of the angelic hosts.

Leader: Even birds make a home and trill love songs to the One who is so majestic and wonderful.

People: Living within the walls of the Almighty's house calls forth melodies of every sort.

Leader: Songs of deliverance bring strength in times of trial.

People: Going through times of difficulty are made easier with the humming of a God song.

Leader: Songs of God help us to remember just how far we have been brought by an unseen force.

People: Songs of courage revive our weak hearts and strengthen our resolve to keep on keeping on!

Leader: The God of Hosts hears and answers our prayers.

People: The God of Yesterday, Today, and Tomorrow provides oil of refreshing for drooping spirits.

Leader: The times spent on the sunlit beaches of the Caribbean do not begin to compare with moments in this sacred sanctuary where the Spirit of God is the light!

People: We scrub the floors, cleanse the toilets, and rub stain in the wood to keep the God-sparkle fresh.

Leader: The sparkle, the twinkle, and the radiance of the stars are generous gifts of God.

People: A day in God's courts is better than a thousand elsewhere. I'd rather serve as an usher in this place than live in a mansion without God! No good thing will God withhold from us!

Offertory Invitation

We are called to pray in the Spirit at all times in every prayer and supplication. We are to keep alert and to always persevere in intercessions for all the people of God. Our giving is a glorious intercession.

Offertory Praise

Jesus, to whom can we go? Only you have the words of eternal life. We have come to believe and to know that you are the Holy One of God. Please receive our gifts and use them that others may come to know. We pray in the name of the Caring Christ.

Benediction

Leader: Finally, go and be strong in Christ Jesus and in the strength of God's power.

People: We have put on the whole armor of God that we may be able to stand against the tricks of the devil.

Leader: Our struggles are not against those of flesh and blood, but against the ruler of this present world.

People: We will stand!

Leader: And having done all you know, stand! God the Truth, Jesus Christ the Righteous, and the Strength of the Holy Spirit undergird us!

People: Hallelujah and amen.

PROPER 17 · SUNDAY BETWEEN AUGUST 28 AND SEPTEMBER 3

Song of Solomon 2:8–13
Psalm 45:1–2, 6–9
James 1:17–27
Mark 7:1–8, 14–15, 21–23

Call to Worship

Leader: The Beloved comes, leaping over mountains, bounding over hills.
People: My Beloved speaks and calls me to arise and come away.
Leader: The flowers appear, the time of singing has come, and the voice of the turtledove is heard.
People: The fig tree puts forth, the vines release, and the fragrance of love is here.
Leader: Arise, Love calls us from labor to re-creation.
People: We have come away to worship and sing love songs.

Call to Confession

We must understand this, beloved—we are to be quick to listen, slow to speak, slow to anger, for anger does not produce the righteousness of God. Therefore, in this time of confession we can rid ourselves of all that comes from wickedness.

Confession

God, it is from within that we have discovered wellsprings of evil. Every sort of dirty intent is buried within our hearts. These have caused us to sin. Forgive us. Cleanse us. Restore us to the state of being "the beloved" to you. We pray in the name of Jesus Christ.

Responsive Reading

Leader: I wish I could rap and rhyme.
People: Words are inadequate to express our hearts.
Leader: Poems and love songs don't touch the reality of what God deserves from our lips.

People: God has been better than best, better than good, and is most assuredly the Most High bomb!

Leader: Since talk and music cannot describe our praise, perhaps we can fight to show our gratitude.

People: We have been equipped with God's armor. We have swords, shields, and helmets at hand.

Leader: God loves righteousness and hates wickedness. Our warrior equipment is only to fight the enemy of our soul. We are to win this war with Love.

People: Our heart is the throne of God. Our will is submitted, oiled with gladness and compassion.

Leader: The fragrance of your prayers is returned upon you. You shall inhabit vast spaces and be given glad hearts.

People: Those we have served will serve us. Honor belongs to us. Treasures are laid up for us by God's right hand. The shackles are off our feet. The chains are broken. We will dance and celebrate.

Offertory Invitation

Every generous act of giving, with every perfect gift, is from above, coming down from God. Our God is not subject to change. Because of God's faithfulness we have been given birth by the word of truth and grace to labor by power from above. We are blessed to share so that others might be won.

Offertory Praise

God, we are making every attempt to be doers of your word and not hearers who deceive themselves. We have given in response to your word. Please accept our gifts, presented with meekness by the power of the Living Word, who has saved our soul and in whose name we pray.

Benediction

Leader: Go into the world, being quick to listen, slow to speak, and slow to anger.

People: We leave to practice God's perfect law of liberty and to be doers of God's Word.

Leader: Go into the world, being willing to persevere.

People: We leave to work the work of the One who sent us.

Leader: The Dominion, the Truth, and the Power go before us!

People: Hallelujah and amen.

PROPER 18 · SUNDAY BETWEEN SEPTEMBER 4 AND SEPTEMBER 10

Proverbs 22:1–2, 8–9, 22–23
Psalm 125
James 2:1–10, (11–13), 14–17
Mark 7:24–37

Call to Worship

Leader: The God of good names desires an audience.
People: The God of favor wants to open doors and make ways for us.
Leader: The God of the just wants to open our eyes so we may perfectly see.
People: We gather this day to reap a harvest of blessings. Praise the God of the harvest.

Call to Confession

We do well if we really fulfill the royal law, "You shall love your neighbor as yourself." But we know that we continue to show partiality to those who have more and seem to be powerful. Therefore, we have sinned. We are convicted by God's law as transgressors. This is our time of confession.

Confession

God of all, to thee we raise this, our prayer of humble confession. Of all folks we know better than to show favoritism. Yet we continue to dishonor the poor by our attitude of neglect. You have chosen the poor in this world to be rich in faith and heirs to your realm. Forgive us our sin. We pray in the name of the Risen Christ.

Words of Assurance

Blessed are the poor in spirit. Theirs is the realm of God. This is good news.

Responsive Reading

Leader: Yesterday, today, and tomorrow God remains the same.
People: Our surrounding God is worthy of trust.
Leader: We are in God's impenetrable care.

People: Our encircling God is with us from time past until time is no more.
Leader: The appearance of evil being the victor in our lives is only a demonic lie.
People: The eye of God roams the earth, seeking those who refuse to participate in wrong.
Leader: Regardless of our circumstance, it is expected by God that we will reach out to others and to lift as we climb.
People: God is lavish in bestowing benefits to all who are upright in their motives.
Leader: It is God who helps us.
People: It is God who leads us to do the right thing and to hang with God's ways.
Leader: Everyone who forsakes God and follows the politically correct ways of the world will be destroyed.
People: God covers us with great grace and amazing shalom!

Offertory Invitation

Whoever keeps the whole law but fails in one point has become accountable for all of it. Living good means giving as well. It's time now for our offering.

Offertory Praise

Jesus Christ, you have done everything well. It is by your goodness that the deaf have been made to hear and the mute to speak. It is only by your grace that you have touched our hearts to share. Now, receive these our gifts as a token of our thanks, we pray.

Benediction

Leader: Go, showing mercy in the world.
People: Mercy triumphs over judgment.
Leader: Go, being active in your faith.
People: Deeds triumph over words.
Leader: Go, being generous with your love.
People: Giving triumphs over receiving.
Leader: God the beneficent, Jesus Christ the just, and the Holy Spirit work in us both the will and the ability to do every good work.
People: Hallelujah and amen.

PROPER 19 · SUNDAY BETWEEN SEPTEMBER 11 AND SEPTEMBER 17

Proverbs 1:20–33
Psalm 19
James 3:1–12
Mark 8:27–38

Call to Worship

Leader: A word to the wise is sufficient.
People: A woman named Wisdom seeks to have an affair with us.
Leader: A word to the wise is sufficient.
People: A woman named Wisdom cries out in the public streets.
Leader: A word to the wise is sufficient.
People: Speak, Wisdom. We have gathered to listen and to truly hear the words that will make us wise.

Call to Confession

Wisdom has been calling to us. Today she cries, "Because I have called and you refused, have stretched out my hand and no one heeded, and because you have ignored all my counsel and would have none of my reproof, I will laugh at your calamity. I will mock when panic strikes you like a whirlwind and distress and anguish come upon you." This is a difficult saying to hear. It calls us to confession.

Confession

God, we have hated knowledge and have not chosen to give you due reverence. We have walked away from your counsel and tried instead to be politically correct. Today Wisdom has gotten our attention. Forgive us our sin. Remove your reproach. Restore us to right relationship, we pray in the name of Knowledge above Knowledge.

Words of Assurance

Waywardness kills the simple and the complacency of fools destroys them. But those who listen to the wisdom of God will be secure. They will live at ease without dread of disaster. This is our good news.

Responsive Reading

Leader: The exhibition tour of the Almighty is on.

People: Exquisite mornings beckon us to awake. And dazzling night lights twinkle in full array.

Leader: Articulation is not necessary. There are no adequate words to record their testimonies.

People: Silence speaks in booming voices as Mother Nature testifies.

Leader: With more mastery than a young groom, and more beauty than a true bride, daybreak and moonlight keep track without benefit of time clocks.

People: The Word of God pulls all the pieces of our fragmented lives together.

Leader: God's life signs point the way to life with abundance!

People: The Holy Scriptures are a map, a guide, showing us how to fully live.

Leader: God's way is plain.

People: God's reputation is solid.

Leader: God's wisdom is a worldwide gift to humankind.

People: More precious than jewels, more rich than ripe, sweet fruit, God's Word is secure.

Leader: Treasure ships nor vaults hold the vast riches of God's Word.

People: The Word of God will guide even fools.

Leader: God, teach us how to hear and to understand.

People: God's directions provide fresh starts.

Leader: God, enrich us with new beginnings.

People: Wash us in the sunlight of your fresh Word. Let the word of our mouths and the meditation of our hearts always be acceptable to you, O Lord, our rock and our redeemer.

Offertory Invitation

Indeed, what can we give in return for our life? Those who are ashamed of Jesus Christ and his words in this adulterous and sinful generation, of them he will be ashamed in the glory of God. Let us show that we are not ashamed by the way we share our gifts.

Offertory Praise

By our giving we make attempts to show that we know that Jesus Christ is the Messiah, the son of the Benevolent. God, please receive these, our gifts in the name of the One who gave his life for us and the world.

Benediction

Leader: Go to be followers of Jesus Christ.

People: We leave to deny ourselves, take up our cross, and follow the Lamb.

Leader: Those who want to save their lives will lose them.

People: We leave to give our lives for the sake of the gospel. For what would it profit us to gain the whole world and forfeit our lives?

Leader: Go in the strength of the Most High God, the adoration of Jesus Christ, and the victory of the Holy Spirit.

People: Hallelujah and amen.

PROPER 20 · SUNDAY BETWEEN SEPTEMBER 18 AND SEPTEMBER 24

Proverbs 31:10–31
Psalm 1
James 3:13–4:3, 7–8a
Mark 9:30–37

Call to Worship

Leader: This is the Church of the Living God.
People: We are the Bride of Christ.
Leader: We are more precious than a rare collection of jewels.
People: Jesus Christ trusts that we will be diligent and faithful in our every effort.
Leader: Strength and dignity are our clothing. We can laugh in the days to come.
People: We open our mouths with wisdom and kindness is on our tongue.
Leader: We are the children of the ancestors who followed the ways of God.
People: We continue to praise God for their faithfulness in teaching us the way.
Leader: We are the Bride of Christ.
People: We are the Church of the Living God, gathered to worship in spirit and truth.

Call to Confession

Who is wise and has understanding among us? We are to show by our good life that our deeds are done with the gentleness born of wisdom. Yet, we know that there is bitter envy and selfish ambition among us. We cannot be boastful nor false to the truth. It is our time to confess.

Confession

God, the conflicts and disputes among us are too many. We want things and crave what is not good for us. There is a war within us that manifests as a war between us. We engage in ways that are not pleasing to you or evidence that we are following your way. Forgive us our sin. Give us your lasting shalom, we pray in the name of Christ.

Words of Assurance

A harvest of righteousness is sown in peace for those who make peace. When we submit ourselves unto God and resist the devil, evil has to flee from us. Yet, when we draw near to God, God will draw near to us. This is our good news.

Responsive Reading

Leader: Stay away from fools!
People: Don't follow the advice of the community idiot!
Leader: Don't hang out with those who have no shame.
People: But follow after those who role model Christ-like behaviors.
Leader: Be a mentor of those who exhibit consistent godly wisdom.
People: Check out the lifestyles, not of the rich and famous!
Leader: We will pattern our lives after those who have prospered and retained a good name and solid reputation.
People: Lifestyles may vary among those who are unfaithful.
Leader: But even the gain of economic resources cannot change those with determined minds to follow God.
People: God watches over the way of those who seek to do the right thing. But the way of the wicked will soon come to a fatal end.

Offertory Invitation

The Bride of Christ opens her hands to the poor and reaches out her hands to the needy. She is not afraid of circumstances for she is more than prepared. Our sharing keeps the Bride of Christ ready to offer help around the world.

Offertory Praise

Charm is deceitful, beauty is vain, but the Church who gives reverence to God is to be praised. God will give her a share in the fruit of her hands and her works will praise her in the city and beyond. God, we your people ask you to receive these, the fruit of our hands in the name of the Vine of Life.

Benediction

Leader: Remember, whoever wants to be first must be last of all and servant of all.
People: We leave to be servants in the name of the Christ.
Leader: Whoever welcomes even a child in his name welcomes the Trinity.
People: We leave to be little children, alive with the love of God.
Leader: God the Welcome, Jesus the Chief Servant, and the Holy Spirit escort us along the journey.
People: Hallelujah and amen.

PROPER 21 · SUNDAY BETWEEN SEPTEMBER 25 AND OCTOBER 1

Esther 7:1–6, 9–10, 9:20–22
Psalm 124
James 5:13–20
Mark 9:38–50

Call to Worship

Leader: The God who grants petitions is prepared to hear our case.
People: The Chief Judge is seated to be heard.
Leader: The God who provides compensation for wrongs waits to grant justice.
People: We approach the bar seeking grace and mercy.
Leader: There is no greater love than that God has for us who seek an audience this morning.
People: We have come to offer praise and thanksgiving for life, redemption, and salvation.

Call to Confession

Are any among us suffering? We should pray. Are any of us cheerful? We should sing songs of praise. Are any of us sick? We should call for the elders of the church and have them pray, anointing them with oil in the name of Jesus. The prayer of faith will save the sick, and God will raise them up; and anyone who has committed sins will be forgiven. In order that God might minister to our needs, let us take the time to confess.

Confession

God, this morning, we pause to confess our sin before you and to each other. We have sinned and neglected to follow your commands. We have paid attention to our feelings and desires more than to your Word. Like Haman, we deserve death. Forgive us. Save us from ourselves, we pray in the name of the One who died in our place.

Words of Assurance

My brothers and sisters, when anyone of us wanders from the truth and is brought back by confession, a sinner's soul is saved from death. For God's love covers a multitude of sins. This is our good news.

Responsive Reading

Leader: This is a continuing repeat story!
People: There are always those who want to totally annihilate us and wipe us from history.
Leader: If it had not been for God on our side, when our enemies plotted and planned, we would have been completely wiped out.
People: They have utilized misinformation, under-education and unsanitary housing.
Leader: We have been used as guinea pigs in medical research or not been treated at all.
People: Every wicked plot, plan, and scheme imaginable has been devised to destroy us.
Leader: But God has saved us.
People: This is a marvel even to us.
Leader: Without sufficient numbers to wage war, without enough political clout to change systems, and without equal access to information used against us, we have not been given by God as prey to the wicked.
People: Every time it seems that we are almost down for the count, God provides another way of escape.
Leader: Who is our help?
People: Our help and our hope is only in the strong name of the Sovereign God who created heaven and earth.

Offertory Invitation

We enter into another season of harvest. God has been lavish in generosity. This is our time of ingathering, where our sharing will turn sorrow into gladness and mourning into holidays. Around the world, our giving will send gifts of food and presents to the poor. Let us honor God with our gifts.

Offertory Praise

God, Queen Esther took a risk and gave all she had to save her people. Like her, we extend ourselves to offer a hand up around the world. Receive these gifts in the name of the Greatest Gift.

Benediction

Leader: Go, knowing that whoever is not against us is for us.

People: We leave to offer cups of cold water in the name of Christ.

Leader: Go, knowing that what you give will be multiplied in its return to you.

People: We leave, covenanting not to be a stumbling block in the world.

Leader: Go, being the salt of the world.

People: We leave to change the world by our lives, our conduct, and our conversation.

Leader: God the Well of Life, Jesus the Bread of Life, and the Shalom of the Holy Spirit establish our going until we meet again.

People: Hallelujah and amen.

PROPER 22 · SUNDAY BETWEEN OCTOBER 2 AND OCTOBER 8

Job 1:1, 2:1–10
Psalm 26
Hebrews 1:1–4, 2:5–12
Mark 10:2–16

Call to Worship

Leader: We bless the God of integrity!
People: Among rumors, gossip, and innuendo, this God calls us to uplift truth.
Leader: We bless the God of steadfast love!
People: In the midst of false friends, smiling faces that are masks, and betrayal, this God demands that we remain faithful and loving.
Leader: We bless the God of boundless mercy!
People: Despite yesterday's lack and tomorrow's uncertainty, this day we come to offer worship to the One who keeps every promise!

Call to Confession

Satan has gone out from the presence of God and inflicted loathsome burdens upon us. It was God who offered up our name! How have we held up during the storms that afflicted us last week? Most of us have not maintained our integrity like Job. This is our time to confess.

Confession

God, we are like the wife of Job. When bad things happen we feel that you have left us and our faith falters. We never stop to consider that you have allowed evil to tempt us so that we would know the reality of our faith. Forgive us our sin. Keep us from being foolish fault finders, we pray in the name of Truth.

Words of Assurance

In good times and in bad, God is present to us. As a matter of fact, God is rooting for us, wanting us to hold on and to hold out. When we can't find it within ourselves to carry on, God will carry us through. This is good news.

Responsive Reading

Leader: Trust and truth are on trial.
People: We talk a good game. The truth is often far from our talk.
Leader: The proof is in the pudding. God is testing our hearts and our minds.
People: As God examines us, it is with a scrutiny that embarrasses.
Leader: It's nice to talk about "those" evildoers.
People: It feels good to point the finger at others.
Leader: But the real deal is that too often we are hypocrites, doing worse than "them"!
People: It's time to wash our hands and come clean before God's altar.
Leader: God, how we long to bust loose with praise songs and dance like there are no shackles on our feet!
People: Yet we need you to sweep over our souls again so that we do not end up with the evildoers.
Leader: Our integrity is on the line!
People: We're straight up about walking the talk. We will bless the name of the Living God with our lives!

Offertory Invitation

Jesus is not ashamed to call us brothers and sisters, saying "I will proclaim your name in the midst of the congregation." And we are not ashamed to show our appreciation by sharing our gifts as a congregation. For in our giving we help other brothers and sisters.

Offertory Praise

"Let the little children come unto me," said Jesus. "Do not stop them; for it is to such that the realm of God belongs." We have given to help all children come to Jesus, in whose name we pray.

Benediction

Leader: Divorce is not an option in God's relationship with us!
People: We leave secured in the love of God.
Leader: Separation is not an issue when we talk about our covenant with God.
People: We leave knowing that God's Word is trustworthy.
Leader: The Eternal God, the Saving God, and the Keeping God enfold us with joy.
People: Hallelujah and amen.

PROPER 23 · SUNDAY BETWEEN OCTOBER 9 AND OCTOBER 15

Job 23:1–9, 16–17
Psalm 22:1–15
Hebrews 4:12–16
Mark 10:17–31

Call to Worship

Leader: The Invisible Presence seeks us.
People: We have a need to see God.
Leader: The Majesty and the Glory are here.
People: We have a desire to talk with God.
Leader: The Invincible Force is among us.
People: Sovereign God, meet our needs as we worship.

Call to Confession

Like Brother Job we come with bitter complaints and serious groans. For many of us God has been silent and seemingly absent this past week. We gather this morning on sheer hopes and feeble faith. We cannot hide our realities from God. This is our time to confess.

Confession

"Oh, that we knew where to find you, God, that we might come to your dwelling. We would lay our case before you and present our arguments with flair. We want to learn what you would answer us and to understand what you would say to us. Would you contend with us in the greatness of your power? Or would you give heed to us?" Like Job, we cannot find you. There are times when we simply want to vanish. Yet we cannot hide from you. So, forgive us our sin. Fix us to see your face, we pray in the name of the Redeemer.

Words of Assurance

Jesus, the Son of God, helps us to hold fast to our confession. For we do not have a high priest who is unable to sympathize with our weaknesses, but we have one who in every respect has been tested as we are, yet without sin. Therefore, we have approached the throne of grace with boldness. Now, we have been promised to receive mercy and to find grace to help in our time of need. Certainly this is good news!

Responsive Reading

Leader: What's up? What's up, God? Why have you walked away?
People: Tears are constant. Groaning is endless. Days are horrible. Nights are worse.
Leader: Why is there no answer, God?
People: Word is that you are holy and sitting on a throne.
Leader: We know that you came to the rescue of the ancestors and delivered them.
People: You heard them on the slave ships and in the cotton fields.
Leader: You lifted them from degradation and shame.
People: But we are seemingly left alone, scorned and despised.
Leader: We are being mocked. People are looking at us in our great despair.
People: Have you dumped us, God? This is the word on the streets!
Leader: Your indifference is appalling! It feels as if you really do not care.
People: We didn't ask to be born black and then to be enslaved.
Leader: Yet, our ancestors have taught us to trust in you.
People: A Mack truckload of troubles has been dumped on us.
Leader: Wild dogs are running lose in our communities and even our homes.
People: We are like wax museum pieces, ready to melt in the heat of destruction.
Leader: Our tongues stick to the roof of our dry mouths as we try to sing praises.
People: We need your immediate attention! This feels like a living hell.

Offertory Invitation

Remember the rich young ruler who tried to hold up the rules he kept as opposed to sharing his wealth with the poor. Jesus did not excuse him.

Neither are we excused. This is our time to share what we have received with others.

Offertory Praise

God, your promise is that when we give to help the poor, we have treasure in heaven. We thank you for the gift of Jesus who came to earth that we might become rich in you. Receive these our gifts, given in his name and for his greater glory, we pray.

Benediction

Leader: The Word of God is living and active.
People: It is sharper than any two-edged sword, piercing until it divides soul from spirit.
Leader: The Word of God judges the thoughts and intentions of our hearts.
People: We leave to be the living and active word in the world.
Leader: God the Word, Jesus the Incarnate One, and the Holy Spirit journey with us.
People: Hallelujah and amen.

PROPER 24 · SUNDAY BETWEEN OCTOBER 16 AND OCTOBER 22

Job 38:1–7 (34–41)
Psalm 104:1–9, 24, 35c
Hebrews 5:1–10
Mark 10:35–45

Call to Worship

Leader: The Cloud Maker and the Water Giver summon us.
People: The Lighting and the Thunder have called us.
Leader: The Mind of the Universe seeks us.
People: The Provider of Every Blessing is here. And we have gathered to offer praise.

Call to Confession

In the days of his flesh, Jesus offered up prayers and supplications, with loud cries and tears, to the One who was able to save him from death. He was heard because of his reverent submission. This is our time to submit with confession.

Confession

Eternal God, like Job we thought we wanted an audience with you. But the truth is that we cannot stand to be questioned by you. We have sinned. We have done evil in your sight. We need forgiveness. We ask for mercy in the name of your son, Jesus Christ.

Words of Assurance

Although Jesus was a Son, he learned obedience through what he suffered; and having been made perfect, he became the source of eternal salvation for all who obey him. This is good news.

Responsive Reading

Leader: My soul gives praise to the Most High.
People: God is great and deserves to be praised.

Leader: The wonder of God is brighter than the sun.
People: The heavens span the skies in glory.
Leader: The oceans sing for joy and the winds whisper praise.
People: Fire and flames give forth exultation.
Leader: Earth has a firm foundation because of the Divine Architect.
People: Mountains, valleys, rivers, and springs have boundaries set in the beginning.
Leader: Animals, birds, and creeping things all offer praise to the Creator.
People: God is more than awesome!
Leader: We pray that our songs are pleasing to the ear of God.

Offertory Invitation

Whoever wishes to be great must first learn how to serve. Now is the time for the service of giving. Let's be generous in our sharing.

Offertory Praise

God, Jesus did not come to be served, but to serve. We are so appreciative that he gave his life as a ransom for many. Please use these, our gifts, in his service and in his name, we pray.

Benediction

Leader: Go to speak honestly with God in all your conversations this week.
People: We go seeking to hear and to see God in the challenges and the struggles ahead.
Leader: Go, encouraged by the fact that God is gentle, understanding, and caring in every way.
People: We leave to wrestle with the issues and to be comforted by God's presence.
Leader: God the Mystery, Jesus the Suffering Servant, and the Holy Spirit keep us empowered till we meet again.
People: Hallelujah and amen.

PROPER 25 · SUNDAY BETWEEN OCTOBER 23 AND OCTOBER 29

Job 42:1–6, 10–17
Psalm 34:1–8 (19–22)
Hebrews 7:23–28
Mark 10:46–52

Call to Worship

Leader: God is beyond comprehension.
People: Great is the Lord and greatly will be praised.
Leader: God is all wise and all knowing.
People: Great is the Lord and greatly will be praised.
Leader: God is the ultimate answer to all of our questions.
People: Great is the Lord who is high and lifted up in our time of worship.

Call to Confession

Jesus is our high priest. He alone is able for all time to save those who approach God through him, since he lives to make intercession for us. This is our call to confession.

Confession

God, it is fitting that we should have a high priest, holy, blameless, undefiled, separated from sinners, and exalted above the heavens. For unlike other high priests, he has no need to offer sacrifices day after day. He did this once for all when he offered himself for our sin. Forgive us for our sin. Help us to accept his atonement and to live the abundant life, we pray in the name of Jesus Christ.

Words of Assurance

God so loved the world until the Only Begotten Son was given to redeem us and offer us brand new life. As God restored Job's fortunes, so God restores our relationship through our confession. This is good news.

Responsive Reading

Leader: Call out a shout for God with me!
People: Word up! There's reason for giving it up for our Living Large God.

Leader: This is the God who has heard our feeble cries.

People: This is the God who has come to rescue us from dangers seen and unseen.

Leader: God is so splendid that even our worst fears have been calmed.

People: God's power is so awesome that hard times have to back up for the blessings.

Leader: There are angels assigned by God to be our bodyguards.

People: Warring angels are dispatched to kick tale and take no names!

Leader: O, taste and see that our God is good.

People: Trouble is on every side!

Leader: And a certain rescue is guaranteed from every one!

People: The wicked will certainly die.

Leader: Those who waste their time and energy on our demise are already condemned.

People: We call out a shout for God, who is a mighty refuge in life's storms.

Offertory Invitation

Aunt Jemima is a name we know from syrup and cereal. But the first Jemima was the beautiful daughter of Job, and sister to Keziah and Keren-happuch. They were gifts from God for Job's righteousness in the face of severe testing. We can be generous with our giving for we know that the record is true; we cannot beat God's repayment plan.

Offertory Praise

God, you gave Brother Job twice as much as he had before his time of testing. We offer you these gifts, for we appreciate the way you multiply. Please bless not only us but the receivers of our sharing, we pray in the name of the Christ.

Benediction

Leader: Take heart! The journey behind us is over.

People: Jesus, Son of David, have mercy on us.

Leader: Get up! Do something with every tomorrow. The journey is before us.

People: Jesus, Son of David, have mercy on us.

Leader: Jesus is calling us! Throw off whatever has kept you bound.

People: Jesus, Son of David, have mercy on us.

Leader: Go in peace! Our faith in the Triune God will take us through.

People: Hallelujah and amen.

PROPER 26 · SUNDAY BETWEEN OCTOBER 30 AND NOVEMBER 5

Ruth 1:1–18
Psalm 146
Hebrews 9:11–14
Mark 12:28–34

Call to Worship

Leader: The tale of two women calls us to worship.
People: We have come to hear a word from God.
Leader: The tale of sisterhood demands our attention.
People: We are here in need of fresh bread for our souls.
Leader: The tale of being hungry in the land of bread will speak to our need.
People: The tale of two women searching for and finding God is praiseworthy. Bread of Life, feed us until we want no more!

Call to Confession

Jesus Christ entered once for all into the Holy Place, not with the blood of goats and calves, but with his own blood, thus obtaining eternal redemption for us. When we sin, we negate his blessed sacrifice. Let us worship through confession.

Confession

God, we pray that the blood of Christ, who through the eternal Spirit offered himself without blemish to you, will purify our conscience from dead works. Forgive our sin. Help us to worship you in spirit and in truth, we ask in the Savior's name.

Words of Assurance

Our Sovereign God is one. We have the power and the ability to love our God, with all our heart, with all our soul, and with all our mind and strength. And, through the Holy Spirit we are given the additional blessing to be able to love our neighbor as we love ourselves. This is good news.

Responsive Reading

Leader: God is in charge! Let the world take notice.
People: All day long we lift our voices in praise.

Leader: Trust is a big factor in our relationship.

People: We have learned not to trust in mortals. We trust only the One who can deliver.

Leader: The Creator has shown off big time with both the heavens and the earth.

People: We know that every promise of God will be kept.

Leader: Prisoners are set free. Blinded eyes are opened.

People: Broken spirits are mended, for God loves the oppressed.

Leader: The all-watching eye of God is forever alert to our smallest movements.

People: Those who feel that no one has their backs can depend upon God.

Leader: The reign of God is forevermore.

People: The praise of those who have intimate knowledge of God will last just as long.

Offertory Invitation

Jesus has already said that we are commanded to love God and to love our neighbor as we love ourselves. There is no argument. The time of sharing our love is at hand.

Offertory Praise

God, we have always been a sharing people. It is in our nature to bless others in the community. Now we give to the wider community. We ask that you would receive these gifts and bless these gifts that the love you have shared with us will spread far and wide. We pray in the name of the Ultimate Giver.

Benediction

Leader: Ruth told Naomi, "Do not press me to leave you or to turn back from following you!"

People: "Where you go, I will go. Where you lodge, I will lodge. Your people shall be my people and your God my God. Where you die, I will die and there I will be buried. Not even death shall part us."

Leader: Ruth's declaration was a forerunner of Christ's love for us. Go knowing you are never alone. God, the Promise Keeper, Jesus Christ the Promise, and the Holy Spirit are constant companions.

People: Hallelujah and amen.

PROPER 27 · SUNDAY BETWEEN NOVEMBER 6 AND NOVEMBER 12

Ruth 3:1–5, 4:13–17
Psalm 127
Hebrews 9:24–28
Mark 12:38–44

Call to Worship

Leader: The bitter, the resentful, and the hateful are welcomed to this house.
People: God, our security, is present for us.
Leader: The lonely, the widowed, the divorced, and the never married are welcomed to this house.
People: God, our redeemer, is present for us.
Leader: The childless, the addicted, and the ill are welcomed to this house.
People: God, who knows our longings, is present for us.
Leader: This is the house called by God's name. All are welcomed here.
People: We come to offer worship and praise.

Call to Confession

The Winnowing Savior longs to meet us at the threshing floor! We can come and uncover our wounds and our needs. In this place we don't need masks of pretense. God knows us each by name. This is our time of confession.

Confession

God, we have said it so lightly, "All that you tell us we will do." Then, we go and forget what you said! Or we remember and chose to do just the opposite. Then our life becomes bitter and we don't want to accept responsibility. But we have come to confess our sin. We have come to repent of our willful separation from your ways. Forgive us in the name of Amazing Love, we pray.

Words of Assurance

Christ did not enter a sanctuary made by human hands, a mere copy of the true one. But he entered into heaven itself, now to appear in the presence of God on our behalf. This is our good news.

Responsive Reading

Leader: Draw up the plans. Lay a firm foundation.

People: If God is not the builder we are working against ourselves!

Leader: Get the best security system available. Put up the most decorative burglar bars.

People: If God is not your night guard, you might as well sleep with the doors wide open!

Leader: Worry and stress. Be anxious and filled with fears about your economic situation.

People: That doesn't solve a thing. God gives sweet rest to those who have little.

Leader: We are the offspring of great people.

People: We have survived the Middle Passage and continuing slavery!

Leader: The ancestors stand on heaven's balcony, watching and cheering our progress.

People: We have given them much to celebrate. We are their heritage. Our achievements are a blessing to their lives on earth. They will not be put to shame. Thanks be unto God.

Offertory Invitation

A poor widow came into the Temple and put in two small copper coins, which were worth a penny. Jesus called his disciples and said, "I tell you, this poor widow has put in more than all those who are contributing to the treasury." Jesus is yet watching. It is time for us to give.

Offertory Praise

God, many people are blessed to contribute out of their abundance. But we have given sacrificially out of what we could use to live on ourselves. Thank you for the privilege of giving. Receive these, our gifts, in the name of the One Who Watches.

Benediction

Leader: Just as it is appointed for mortals to die once, and after that the judgment, so Christ, having been offered once to bear the sins of many, will appear a second time, not to deal with sin, but to save us who are eagerly waiting for him. Go waiting. Go watching. Go living as Jesus Christ taught. The power is ours.

People: Thanks be unto God.

PROPER 28 · SUNDAY BETWEEN NOVEMBER 13 AND NOVEMBER 19

1 Samuel 1:4–20
Psalm 16
Hebrews 10:11–14 (15–18), 19–25
Mark 13:1–8

Call to Worship

Leader: God is waiting to hear a sincere petition like Hannah's.
People: We come to the God of pregnant possibilities.
Leader: It seemed as if all hope was gone. She was frustrated and in grief.
People: We come seeking the God of mighty miracles.
Leader: God heard her prayer and granted her heart's desire.
People: This is the very same God that we want to worship!

Call to Confession

When Christ offered for all times a single sacrifice for sins, he sat down at the right hand of God. It is there he makes intercession for us. This is our time of confession.

Confession

The Holy Spirit has testified to us saying, "This is the covenant that I will make with them after those days, says the Lord; I will put my laws in their hearts, and I will write them on their minds. I will remember their sins and lawless deeds no more. For where there is forgiveness of these, there is no longer any offering for sin." God, despite your provisions, we have sinned. Forgive us. Write upon our hearts anew, we pray in the name of the Covenant Signer in Blood.

Responsive Reading

Leader: We live in a time when so little makes sense!
People: The things we thought were secure are crumbling away.
Leader: Without the loving presence of God we have no hope.
People: Our relationship with God is all that we have to depend upon.

Leader: We are not into God-shopping!
People: There is only one God, and Most High is that righteous name.
Leader: We have chosen sides. Our territory is clearly marked.
People: We won't retreat. We won't back up. We stake our lives on God.
Leader: Give honor to God, who is counselor and teacher.
People: We pledge allegiance to the all-wise God.
Leader: Keeping it real with God will put joy in our feet and laughter in our hearts.
People: We refuse to go to hell! Life on this side has been no piece of cake!
Leader: We have won the big lotto!
People: Our life was at stake and God drew us out of death's pit. We're on the right road now! There is no turning around!

Offertory Invitation

Since we have a great priest over the house of God, let us approach with a true heart in full assurance of faith that whatever we give, God will multiply and use to further glory. Let us give.

Offertory Praise

God, we are living in the end times. Nations have risen against nations, kingdom against kingdom; there are earthquakes, floods in various places, and world famines. We are giving in hopes of your realm coming with our help. Receive these gifts in the name of the One Who Is Coming.

Benediction

Leader: Go into the world, holding fast to the confession of our hope without wavering, for Jesus Christ, who has promised, is faithful.
People: We leave considering how to provoke one another to love and good deeds, not neglecting to meet together and encouraging one another all the more.
Leader: God the Faithful, Jesus the Hope of Glory, and the Holy Spirit keep us walking the talk!
People: Hallelujah and amen.

PROPER 29 · THE REIGN OF CHRIST
SUNDAY BETWEEN NOVEMBER 20 AND NOVEMBER 26

2 Samuel 23:1–7
Psalm 132:1–12 (13–18)
Revelation 1:4b–8
John 18:33–37

Call to Worship

Leader: Strong One of Israel, we gather in your name.
People: Rock of Israel, in the light of this morning, your praise is upon our lips.
Leader: Everlasting Covenant, it is right and proper that we come into your presence.
People: You are worthy to be lifted, exalted, and worshiped, for you are Sovereign!
Leader: Christ rules!
People: To God be glory!

Call to Confession

Jesus Christ, the faithful witness, the firstborn of the dead, and the ruler of the kings of the earth, has loved us and freed us from our sins by his blood and made us to be a kingdom of priests. Our sin separates us from this heritage of righteousness. It is confession time.

Confession

God, your love for us is so amazing. We continue to struggle with the fact that the Sovereign of Glory dared to come to earth and be born in our skin. We cannot comprehend that he gave up his divinity so that we might share it. We have sinned. We ask for your forgiveness. We ask for restoration that we might be the kingdom of priests you ordained in the beginning. We pray in the name of Christ, the Ruler.

Words of Assurance

God has made with us an everlasting covenant. Our sincere words of confession are accepted and forgiveness is granted according to the covenant relationship. This is good news.

Responsive Reading

Leader: Good leaders are hard to find and their lives are closely watched.
People: David was anointed as king and yet ran for his life for over twelve years.
Leader: King David held fast to the promise of God and never looked back to the sheepfold.
People: His determination was to build a lasting place of worship for God.
Leader: Extraordinary responsibility calls forth extraordinary dedication.
People: David teaches us how to be compassionate under pressure and graceful in trouble.
Leader: God was faithful to David every step of the journey.
People: David's life was a foretaste of the coming Christ.
Leader: David's linage was promised to always inhabit the throne of Zion.
People: We are the offspring of the linage of David.
Leader: It is required by God that those who have power over people administer with justice.
People: Abundant blessings are provided and satisfaction is guaranteed when we follow God's way.
Leader: May the reign of God be complete in us.
People: We have been anointed by God with crowns of gladness, wreaths of joy, and hearts made merry with praise!

Offertory Invitation

Jesus Christ is coming with the clouds; every eye will see him, even those who pierced him; and on his account all the people of the earth will wail. So it is to be. Amen. To insure that all who want to be can be ready, let us prepare our hearts to give.

Offertory Praise

God, your realm is not of this world. You have a realm not prepared by human hands. We want to inhabit it throughout eternity. We have given these gifts in your name and for your glory. May they help your realm to come as we pray in the name of the Soon Coming Ruler.

Benediction

Leader: Go into the world announcing to every "Pilate" that Jesus Christ rules.

People: We leave to be heralds in the earth.

Leader: Go into the world testifying to the benefits received by belonging to Christ's realm.

People: We will sing it, shout it, and tell of the Beneficent One everywhere we go.

Leader: God the Christ Sender, Christ the Ruler, and the Holy Spirit, the Ruler's Announcer, enfold us til we meet again.

People: Hallelujah and amen.

8 · ADDITIONAL SERVICES

ALL SAINTS SUNDAY

NOVEMBER 1 OR THE FIRST SUNDAY IN NOVEMBER

Isaiah 25:6–9
Psalm 24
Revelation 21:1–6a
John 11:32–44

Call to Worship

Leader: God defies death!
People: We want to forget the stench of dead things!
Leader: God is the Author of Life!
People: We don't want to dwell in the stench of dead things!
Leader: God is the Alpha and the Omega!
People: We refuse to be held captive by the stench of dead things!
Leader: New life is guaranteed. New beginnings start now.
People: We have come to worship and bless God for the memories of those now living on the other side.

Call to Confession

Desires crumble. Wishes become crippled. Hopes wither. Dreams fade. The economy declines. Neighborhoods change. We age. Our loved ones die. The stench of dead things can make us crazy and cause us to sin. This is the time of confession.

Confession

God we are waiting for the time when you will swallow up death forever and wipe away the tears from our eyes. That time is not yet! The stench of death is all around us. We are weary with the groaning pains of our misery. We have great difficulty in giving up our holds on the time that is now past. We miss our loved ones. We hold you responsible for our grief. Forgive us our sin. Release us from the stench of death. Give us new life, we pray, in the name of him who rose again!

Words of Assurance

We have a right-now God! This is the God for whom we have waited. Our God has come to save us from the clutches of eternal death. Let us be glad and rejoice in our salvation. New life is ours. This is good news.

Responsive Reading

Leader: God holds the pawn ticket for everything in the world!
People: The Architect of All established mountain and molehill.
Leader: It's all God's territory!
People: Who can dare to call a meeting with the Supreme Designer?
Leader: Who would make a dumb attempt to stand toe to toe with the Almighty?
People: Step to God with clean hands and you will get an audience.
Leader: Step toward God with lies and smack and you won't be heard!
People: God has blessings galore for seekers and searchers.
Leader: God has put out advance notice that pure-hearted company is welcomed, big time!
People: We lift up our hands in surrender. God's in control!
Leader: Like the ancestors we throw open the doors to our hearts by faith.
People: We know what time it is. And we know who controls time!
Leader: The Commander in Chief is in the house.
People: We are on our feet in honor and in praise for the One who gives, the One who takes, and the One who promises eternal life!

Offertory Invitation

Dead things can be resurrected. Jesus has shown us that new life can and will begin. As we share, the stones of death are rolled away for others.

Offertory Praise

God, you know our hearts' intentions and desires. We thank you for taking away the stone that blocked our wanting to know you. We give these gifts that others may come to know. In the name of the Stone Remover, we pray.

Benediction

Leader: Mary and Martha knew our fears of death.

People: Blessed be the One who came late and was right on time!

Leader: They, too, blamed Jesus for the death of their loved one.

People: Blessed be the One who was greatly disturbed and deeply moved by their grief.

Leader: Mary and Martha took Jesus to the grave site.

People: Blessed be the One who turned mourning into a joy-filled celebration!

Leader: Go forth into the world, with death-defying victory in the name of the Glory, the Resurrection, and the Matchless Power.

People: Hallelujah and amen.

THANKSGIVING DAY
FOURTH SUNDAY IN NOVEMBER
Joel 2:21–27
Psalm 126
1 Timothy 2:1–7
Matthew 6:25–33

Call to Worship

Leader: This is a day of glad celebration!
People: We give thanks with grateful hearts.
Leader: This is a day of honoring the harvest.
People: We offer thanksgiving for God's abundant provisions.
Leader: This is a day of family, friends, and feasting.
People: We gather in communion to worship our lavishly generous God.

Call to Confession

First of all, we are urged on this day to give supplications, prayers, inter-cessions, and thanksgivings for everyone and everything. We are called to pray for all who are in authority with high positions, so that we may lead quiet and peaceable lives in all godliness and dignity. This requires that we now spend time in confession.

Confession

Gracious God, once again we gather on a day of national Thanksgiving. We pause to acknowledge that you are God and besides you there is none other. We come confessing our sin. We come asking for forgiveness. We come wanting to be in right relationship with you. Receive our prayers of repentance that we pray in the name of the Sustainer, Christ.

Words of Assurance

It is right and acceptable that we confess in the sight of God our Savior, who desires that everyone be saved and come to the knowledge of the truth. For there is one God and one mediator between God and humankind, Christ Jesus, who gave himself a ransom for us all. This is good news.

Responsive Reading

Leader: It's just too good to be true! We have come a mighty long ways!
People: God just keeps on doing great things, not only for us but even for the beasts of the fields!
Leader: Tiny things are of significance to the Creator. Nothing was left to chance.
People: God's providence and provision is legendary. For we have a collective testimony.
Leader: There are those who cannot believe how we have survived.
People: Our achievements are touted among the nations. For the world knows our story.
Leader: God has done and is doing great things for us.
People: Shackles and chains are broken; we are filled with joy.
Leader: We are also filled with great expectations.
People: Do it again, God. We want an encore!
Leader: God has promised to repay us for all that the destroyer stole.
People: This is a good thing. We celebrate God's precious promises.
Leader: Our tears and prayers have not been in vain.
People: For those who sow in tears reap with shouts of joy.
Leader: Those who have carried heavy burdens and labored in the fields are promoted.
People: It's our time of ingathering. This is our day of celebration!

Offertory Invitation

Therefore I tell you, do not worry about your life, what you will eat or what you will drink, or about your body, what you will wear. Is not life more than food, and the body more than clothing? Look at the birds of they air; they neither sow nor reap nor gather into barns. Yet, God provides for them. Our sharing helps other broken, little birds to eat and to fly. Let's be generous.

Offertory Praise

"The promise of God is that we shall eat in plenty and praise the name of the Lord our God who has dealt wondrously with us. We shall never again be put to shame." For this reason, God, we have given in your honor. Receive these our gifts in the name of Christ, we pray.

Benediction

Leader: Go into the world sharing a harvest of blessings!

People: The soil has done its part. The seeds and grains have produced. The trees have all cooperated. Even the winds and the rains have been poured down on time. Today we leave to participate in God's abundance.

Leader: Go into the world being a harvest of blessings!

People: We leave fully aware that God is in our midst. Our hearts are filled with joy as we go to celebrate our bounty with others.

Leader: God the Horn of Plenty, Jesus the Great Sacrifice, and the Holy Spirit are with us and for us.

People: Thanks be unto the Triune God! Hallelujah and amen!

CHURCH DEDICATIONS

The people enter and sit in silence. There is no music.

The pastor and other participants come from the rear, in procession, as drums begin a soft beat.

After the pastor and participants are seated, the drummers pick up their pace and a line of praise dancers begins to file in carrying crystal pitchers of water and stand before the altar.

Reader: Water is a symbol of new life. Water is a symbol of our new birth. Water is a symbol of purity, cleansing, and sanctification. Water is a gift from God. Today the waters will bless this space, refresh our spirits, and prepare us for God's latter reign. Let us pray.

People: God of Life-giving Waters, bless us today. Sanctify this place and us for your presence. Amen.

The drummers drum as the praise dancers use their hands to sprinkle blessed water all around the sanctuary. They exit from the rear.

Dedication of Altar Cloths

Drums continue softly, as the altar cloths are brought and presented by communion stewards.

Reader: The royal kente was worn by African kings, queens, and royalty. Kente is a symbol of our connection to Mother Africa and her trust in the High God. These paraments or coverings are symbolic of God's love that covers us. God has called us and given us the generous gift of Jesus, whose death covered our sin. Now, the Holy Spirit shields us in our service to God and the world. As we are blanketed by Everlasting Love, we place these coverings to honor our ancestors who are resting in God. We look forward to the day when the communion shared from this table and the Holy Scripture uplifted from this pulpit will be done around God's throne with all the saints. Let us pray. Covering God, as we gently place these woven pieces upon wood made by your divine hand, we ask that you would cover this place with your presence, your power, and your divine peace. Amen.

Coverings are put in place.

Presentation of Candles and Altar Bible

As drums pick up sound, the lit taper and two unlit candles are brought forward by acolytes for presentation.

Reader: Jesus is the Light of the World. He is ever shining in the world. Nothing can retard or prevent the Light of Glory from bursting forth and illuminating our way. This Light guided our journey from the motherland, across the deep and dangerous waters. This Light provided hope in the painful days of our legal enslavement. It is this same Light who continues to offer us hope in times like these. Let us pray. God of Life-changing Light, bless us today. Let your Light shine both in this sanctuary and in our hearts. Amen.

Two candles are placed on the altar and lit with the taper. The candle lighter exits down the aisle as people stand and sing," Jesus is the Light of the World."[12] The drums continue to play as the altar Bible is brought forward and presented.

Reader: The Living Word of God! These sacred Scriptures speak across the ages. These sacred texts tell our story as wandering people without land or temple to call home. These pages record God's promises to us. These pages give us continuing direction for our journey. Let us pray.
People: God of the Inspired Word, write afresh these words upon the tablets of our longing hearts. Let us eat your Word, so we may more fully live. Amen.

Dedication of the Altar Cross

A reading from scripture: 1 Kings 8:22–30

Drums continue as the altar cross is brought forward and presented.

Reader: This former symbol of guilt and shame now represents our salvation. This former symbol of pain and torture now stands for our healing. This former symbol of death and despair now symbolizes for us eternal life, abiding joy, and everlasting peace. This cross points us to our Risen Savior. No grave could hold his body down. No devil from hell could destroy him. The grave was not able to contain him. This cross now reminds us that we must daily choose to pick up our own cross and follow Jesus into new life. Let us pray. God of Yesterday, Today, and Tomorrow, we thank you for the cross of Calvary. It was the emblem of Christ's suffering and shame. He took it for the sake of our salvation. We thank you for this symbol of his unforgettable love for us. Jesus, keep us always near the cross! Amen.

Cross is placed as congregation stands and sings, "Jesus Keep Me Near the Cross,"[13] a cappella.

Confession and Prayer

A reading from Scripture: 1 Kings 8:33–40, 49–53

Community requests and pastoral prayer

Blessing of Music Ministry

As the drums continue a soft beat, the minister of music comes forward and speaks.

Minister of music: The drums have always called us together as a people. The drums speak messages that inform, illustrate, clarify, and even warn of approaching dangers. The drums are important in our history and remind us that we do walk to the beat of a Different Drummer. Today, the drums help us offer praise to our God for the surpassing greatness that has brought us to this hour.

Choir circles the altar rails and begins to sing, "Blessed Be the Name of the Lord,"[14] a cappella.

These are the Levites among us, called by God and set apart for the ministry of praise and worship. We come, along with the musicians, to consecrate ourselves before God. Let us pray. Music Maker God, enjoy our praise! We have come to praise you, Sovereign God! We will praise you, God, in this sanctuary, with the drums (louder beat). With the horns (horns begin to join in). With stringed instruments (guitar and piano begin to join). With the pipes (organ begins to play). With our voices we bless you, O God (choir sings fully). Let everything that has breath, praise God!

Congregation is invited to stand and sing.

After singing, while standing, the congregation is invited to pray.

All: God of Sight and Sound, receive our ministry of joyful praise this day! We offer you ourselves as living sacrifices. We offer you our voices in thankful worship. Prepare us to be holy and faithful sanctuaries for you. In the name of Sweet Harmony, we pray. Amen.

Message

If there is a message (homily) insert here, or insert words from bishop or presiding elder, depending upon your denomination.

Dedication of Offering Plates and Offering

The offering plates are brought forward and presented.

Reader:
God, the greatest Lover
So loved, the greatest degree
The world, the greatest number
That God gave, the most generous act
The only begotten Son, the greatest gift
That whosoever, the greatest opportunity
Believeth, the greatest simplicity
In Christ, the greatest attraction
Should not perish, the greatest promise
But, the greatest difference
Have, the greatest certainty
Eternal life, the greatest possession!

Now, it's our turn to offer back a just portion of what God has blessed us to receive. As these offering plates are presented for dedication to God's service, let our hearts join in prayer.

All: Generous God, we offer our meager thanks for all you have given us. Into these containers will go the fruit of our labors. You give us life, health, and strength. You provide us with minds, skills, talents, and abilities. You open doors of opportunities and many different avenues of blessings. God, we can't beat your giving! Yet, we appreciate the times you allow us to say, "Thank you," in tangible ways. May these plates always bring into this storehouse the gifts of grateful hearts. Bless the plates and us to your continued mission in the world. Amen.

The people bring to God an offering!

Doxology and Blessing of Ushers

Generous God, we offer unto you these gifts. Bless both gift and liberal givers. Bless those with desires to give unto your work of ministry who have no means today. Open wide windows of blessing and doors of opportunity. We ask your divine anointing upon the ministry of the ushers. As they welcome, greet, and seat your people within your house, let them see you in every face, hear you in every voice, and acknowledge you by their smile. In the name of our Giving Savior, we pray with thankful hearts. Amen.

Dedication of Baptismal Font

The pastor comes forward.

Pastor: Sisters and brothers, we have gathered in this place that has become our sanctuary. Thank God for the precious memories of yesterday and praise God for the hope that has brought us all together today in hopes for brighter tomorrows. What has happened here signals the need for our presence in this area. A Holy Ghost fire has now broken out within our hearts. This fire will burn and spread as others are attracted to what is happening in this place. This fire burns because it is the flame of God's Holy Spirit who leads, guides, draws, and sustains. We are not here by accident. We are here because the flame of the Holy has touched us and will touch others. New believers will come here. New converts will need to be baptized here. And new babies will be born into our family here. So we pause now to dedicate our baptismal font (pool/bowl). For every fire requires fresh water!

Drums begin as the choir sings, "Take Me to the Water."[15] Praise dancers bring in fresh crystal pitchers of water and the pastor sprinkles water over the font. Water is then poured in as rejoicing occurs.

Pastor: Saving God, you have given us the waters of baptism. We were nurtured in water, born from water, and sustained by the water you provide. You separated the waters for your people to enter safety and brought forth sweet water for them to drink, from the Rock. We pause to say thank you! May these who will be baptized into your worldwide family always feel and know your love. Let these waters be our symbols of family, community, and unity as others come to die to sin, rise to new life in pardon, and accept this gift of grace and enter into Christ's most holy Church. Amen.

Presentation of Various Symbols and Love Gifts

Pastor: We thank God for the formal symbols that belong in every Christian house of worship. But we recognize that God's church is not a building, but people. You and I are the Church. What gifts will the people render unto God?

The trustees come with a ring of HUGE keys!

Trustee: Pastor, these keys are to open wide the doors of this building for the people of this community. We covenant to do our part and keep the premises in good order so that the world may come to know Jesus in this place. We will endeavor to be good stewards of this wonderful trust from God and to remember that people are more important than bricks.

The pastor receives the keys and places them on altar or presents them to a denominational representative.

The stewards come with a globe.

Stewards: Pastor, this globe reminds us that we have brothers and sisters both around the world and down the street. Everywhere there are people with needs. There is a need for our ministry. We covenant to share the love of Christ with the world, both at home and abroad. We will endeavor to be good stewards and to remember that we serve the whole people of God.

The pastor receives the globe.

Communion stewards or diaconate members (depending upon your denomination) come with plates and glasses.

Steward/deacon: Pastor, we know it was the shed blood of Jesus and his broken body that gave birth to the Church. May these utensils keep us reminded that it was the sacrifice of Jesus that saved us from a burning hell. We covenant to always be prepared to serve this holy meal in order to provide strength and comfort to the people of God.

The pastor receives the elements.

Sunday school superintendent and teachers bring a lamp.

Superintendent/Christian educator: Pastor, we know that for too many years the Lamp of Knowledge was denied to us as a people. Many did not want us to know what a significant role we played in the Bible. Our heritage has taken on new meaning and we covenant to teach our children and to bring them to a saving knowledge of Jesus Christ.

The pastor receives the lamp.

The youth come bringing fresh flowers that have come from bulbs, such as tulips or gladiolas.

Youth: Pastor, we bring the flowers of our youth. We offer our enthusiasm for exploring, discovering, learning, and sharing. May these flowers remind this congregation that what they do with us will help us to come forth from the buds of promise that we are, to full flowers in the faith.

The pastor receives the flowers.

The children come bringing balloons.

Child: Pastor, we come with our joy! We cannot contain it. We want to share joy with the whole church. We will blow into the many tomorrows that you will never see! Church, help us to sail high!

The pastor receives the balloons.

A representative of the missionary and women's work or women's fellowship (or another name, depending upon your denomination) comes forth bringing a pot, plate, and glass.

Woman: Pastor, truly we have come a long way! We work outside the home and do many complex and different jobs. Yet, we recognize that it is part of our nature to want to share with others around food. The kitchen table is a sign of family and sharing friendship. We covenant to help make this new building a home. We bring our laughter and our tears, as well as our abilities to re-create, to start over, and begin all over again with grand style!

The pastor receives the utensils.

The representative of the men's group comes forth bring a hammer, shovel, and push broom.

Man: Pastor, receive these gifts, which indicate that we are God's mighty men! We represent more than a million men who have declared our intention to recover African American communities for God. It is our nature to build, to repair, and to keep things in order. Yet we, too, have come a long way. We covenant to help make this new building a home. We bring our love for our women, our protection for our children, role-modeling for our youth, and our strength of working together to accomplish great things with few words, but with great faith!

The pastor receives the articles.

A city/county representative comes forth bringing a plaque or framed certificate.

Representative: Pastor, this certifies that this church has duly met the requirements for building in this city (county). This testifies to your abilities of properly filing, following, and adhering to building codes. This building is structurally sound, physically fit, and correctly wired to do the ministry before you. Please put this in a prominent place to inform every inhabitant of their safety from shoddy work or inferior products. May God bless all who enter this building. This document testifies that we are yoked with you in service to this community.

The pastor receives the certificate or plaque.

A community representative comes bring a bag of planting soil.

Representative: Pastor, this potting soil is the dirt from the ground. It is just another reminder that from dirt we all came and to dirt we shall return. This potting soil is a symbol that we appreciate _____ (insert church name) deciding to come (return) here and plant (replant) their work in this community. Together, we can plant fresh dreams, fertilize new hopes, watch the Son of God shine upon our efforts, and harvest a rich crop of people committed to excellence for God.

The pastor receives the soil.

A pastor from another denomination comes bringing a jar of virgin olive oil.

Visiting clergy: Pastor, we serve in this ministry together. We may be in different parts of the city; we even belong to different denominations; our styles and forms of worship are different, but we serve the same God. Every church is just another healing station for the people of God. God told us to use fresh pressed, virgin olive oil for anointing. The anointing represents the Holy Spirit who is alive, well, and in this place today. May this oil remind you and the members that you are never alone. Somebody, somewhere is praying for you! For our congregation covenants to be in ministry with you.

The pastor receives the oil.

The pastor calls forth a denominational representative, bishop, or presiding elder, indicating the host of love gifts present around altar,

Pastor: The culmination of all our efforts lie before you. I was given the charge of uniting families. Mission accomplished! I was given the vision, from God, to build (rebuild) a building. Mission accomplished! Today, you have witnessed the dedication and consecration of the saints of God here at _____. We are a loving family. That mission is already accomplished! We are ready, willing, and able to begin the work of ministry, in the name of Jesus Christ. What is your response?

Denominational representative: On behalf of the ancestors, who have gone before us; on behalf of the Mother Church and her pioneers who charted the course for us; on behalf of pastors and members around the world, who work with us; on behalf of our bishop (president, general board of officers (depending upon your denomination)), I charge you to be about the business of winning souls, forming faithful disciples, teaching children, baptizing and dispensing holy sacraments in the name of our Sovereign God. I charge you to open wide these doors to the community, to be diligent in your efforts to bring our youth off the streets and into a saving knowledge of God, their heritage, and their potential. I charge you to teach family values. I charge you to be concerned for the aging, the poor, and the homeless. I charge you to be in mission, both here and abroad. I charge you to be the Church of Jesus, seasoning salt, bright light, and a city set on a hill. Let your work speak for you. And by the life that you live and the service that you give, the world will see Jesus, and come to be saved. What I say to one, I say to all, I charge you to be the Church of Jesus Christ!

Song of Celebration

After singing, with congregation standing:

A reading from scripture: 1 Kings 8:54–51

Benediction and Blessing

Pastor: Leave to be the Church, in the world.
People: We leave with great joy!
Pastor: Leave to be the Church, in this community.
People: We leave with great hope!
Pastor: Leave to be the Church, in your homes.
People: We leave with great anticipation!
Pastor: Leave to be the Church! May the God of Creation surround you, the love of Christ, protect you, and the power of the Holy Spirit energize you for the work ahead.
People: The God of Blackness is with us. The Christ of Darkness shines in us. The Holy Mystery of the Ages watches over us.
Pastor: Go, in Peace.
Unison: Hallelujah and amen!

Drummers begin, praise dancers lead out, and participants follow to joyful sounds and a feast of celebration!

WORSHIP FOR INTERNATIONAL WOMEN'S HISTORY OBSERVANCE

Call to Worship

Leader: The Parent of All Children calls us to gather.
People: We come as women who are daughters, sisters, aunts, and mothers.
Leader: The Parent Who Loves calls us to gather.
People: We come as women who love and need to love.
Leader: The Parent Who Understands calls us to gather.
People: We come as women who have tried to understand.
Leader: The Parent Who Saves calls us to gather.
People: We come looking for salvation for our children. We have run out of methods, strategies, and alternatives. The world seems to be falling apart and our children are being destroyed. We gather to seek help.
Leader: This is the place. This is the time. This is the hour for us and our children.
People: We have gathered to worship and offer praise to the Parent of All Children. Amen.

Hymn of Celebration

Invocation

Leader: Jesus, you completely gave up your divinity and emptied yourself into humanness.
People: You became naked, utterly stripped and bare for us.
Leader: Now you give yourself to us as the Bread of Life.
People: Your completeness sustains us.
Leader: You give yourself to us as the Cup of Consolation.
People: You are the Way, the Truth, the Light, and our Eeternal Hope.
Leader: Jesus Christ, we thank you for being God's Incarnate Love, living in us.
People: We welcome your presence in this place and in us, for we pray in your name.

Call to Confession

There are so many things that we do not understand. Watching the world change so swiftly is frightening. Watching our children destroy and be destroyed is terrifying. Having a war of terrorism brought into our homes is beyond belief. Sometimes we feel helpless. Many times we throw up our hands in despair. We feel that we are in charge of our small worlds, and we forget that the whole wide world is in God's capable hand. Let us confess our sin, which separates us from the Omnipotent One.

Silent Confession

Corporate Confession

Loving Parent, we are women who have been children. We know the pressures and the strain we have placed upon our own parents. Now, we are the women who have birthed children, raised others' children, and longed to have children. We are the women who have aborted children and had to give children up for adoption. We are the women who watch and are concerned about the children in our world. For too long we have tried to come up with the answers. For too long we have taken responsibility for making the world better, safer, and more secure, without realizing that you are the Ultimate Parent. Forgive us our sin. Forgive us for forgetting that you long to be involved in our lives and in the life of every child. Forgive us for forgetting that your heart is broken for the pain and suffering of every child. Forgive us for forgetting that you do have a better idea for the salvation and restoration of your world! Thank you for initiating the Love that has called us here. Restore us and make us whole. For we pray in the name of the Child born to die for our sin. Amen.

Words of Assurance

Jesus Christ, the same yesterday, today, and forever, grants us new life, new strength, and new hope. This is our blessed assurance.

Songs of Celebration

Message

Affirmation

Leader: We are women of God!
People: We are women, created in the image of God!
Leader: We are women of God, given unlimited potential and pregnant possibilities!

People: We are women of God, created, not merely made, but divinely designed!

Leader: We are women of God!

People: We are equal to men, but different from them.

Leader: Our perception, our wit, and our intuition give us discernment beyond our years.

People: Our responsibilities are to perpetuate the world and to care for those who are born.

Leader: We are women of God. When God rested, the rest of creation was left unto us.

People: If a scientist is to discover a new solution to cancer or AIDS, we must birth him or her first.

Leader: If a philosopher is to think of the answer for world peace and future safety, we must birth her or him first.

People: We are the women of God, cocreators in the birthing process.

Leader: Our greatest accountability to the Sovereign is making the world a better place.

People: We will not accept mediocrity! We refuse to bow to subservience!

Leader: The foremothers did it for our survival.

People: It was never ordained by God that we would be enslaved.

Leader: Our inheritance, as women of God, is to take the message of Christ to the world.

People: A woman's seed brought forth Christ. A woman by an old well took his message to her whole town because Jesus told her he was the Messiah. He never told anyone else!

Leader: It was a woman, in a garden, looking for her lost love, who ran into the risen Savior.

People: And Jesus gave her the duty of telling the disciples that the resurrection had occurred!

Leader: We are women of God with unlimited horizons and numerous choices before us.

People: We are women of God, distinct, special, and different.

Leader: We are women, but individuals each one.

People: We are women, but there is no cookie-cutter mold into which we must fit.

Leader: We are women of God, called to ministry in diverse forms, methods, and roles.

People: We are women of God, alive by Christ's blood and empowered by the Holy Spirit to make a difference, make every day count, live out our destiny, and make God look good in every meantime. We are God's women, and that's mighty good news!

Music of Celebration

Call to Offering

(Call the congregation to consider donating both money and "necessary" items to shelters for women.)

Offertory Praise

It is only of divine grace that we find ourselves able to share from our resources. Merciful God, we acknowledge your abundance. We thank you for the gift of sisterhood. We thank you for the love that binds us heart to heart and breast to breast. For as your nurtuing creatures we know how to be generous with our giving. We pray now for every woman and her family who have given, and we pray for every woman and her family who will benefit from our ability to offer you thanks in tangible ways. We ask that you receive our gifts in the name of the One who loved, accepted, called, and sent women with the blessing of hope!

Benediction

Leader: The Womb of Being has gathered us here, met us, and now sends us on our way.
People: This time was for us to listen, to share our stories, and to celebrate ourselves.
Leader: The daughters of the healing God have met.
People: This time was for us to be reminded that healing and wholeness are our portion.
Leader: The daughters of the God of promise have met.
People: The singing, the Living Word, the affirmations all help us to leave this time.
Leader: Go! Live the songs. Be the Word. Remember the affirmations. For God the Creator, Christ the Redeemer, and the Sustaining Holy Spirit go before us and within us until we meet again. Thanks be unto God.
All: Hallelujah and amen!

THE YAM CEREMONY · A CELEBRATION FOR THE BLACK CHURCH

Note: This worship service was designed and created by the author for Black Methodists for Church Renewal Sunday. It has been adapted here for use by any African American congregation.[16] Congregations need to announce early in February that this worship has a heavy emphasis on sweet potatoes. Members should be asked to bring sweet potato pies, cakes, muffins, and cookies, which can be blessed and then shared during the coffee hour. The worship committee should be encouraged to build an altar display featuring many different sizes and shapes of yams to be a focus for the day. Members will be asked to bring their contributions forth before the litany, in order that the congregation can see the many and varied items that yams provide.

Call to Worship

Leader: Today we gather to celebrate the gift we are as African Americans.
People: We celebrate our African roots. We celebrate our spirituality, brought with us to these shores. We celebrate our different ways of being that we share with the wider Church. We celebrate the High God who has traveled with us all of our days.
Leader: Today we gather to celebrate the gift we are as African Americans.
People: We affirm that we are on a journey, often from can't to can. We affirm that "stony the road we trod"[17] with stumbling blocks of racism often blocking our way. We affirm the God has been our help in ages past and is our hope for the years to come.
Leader: Today we gather to celebrate the gift we are as African Americans.
People: We have a song to sing. We have a story to tell. We have our heroes and heroines to recall. We have our own faith journey to share and our own rituals to rehearse. We have a God to praise, we have a Christ to uplift, and we have the Holy Spirit to magnify.
Unison: Today we gather to celebrate the gift we are as African Americans.

Hymn of Praise

"Lift Every Voice and Sing"[18]

Call to Confession

Now is the acceptable time. Today is the day of salvation. With open hearts and repentant spirits, let us turn, in confession, to the Ultimate One, who longs to be in covenant relationship with us. Let us pray.

Confession[19]

Loving God, we are an unfaithful people. You created us in your image and breathed into us the breath of life. We have marred your image and done deeds of death to ourselves and to others. Have mercy on us. Blot out our sin and forgive us. Purge us and we will be clean. Wash us and we will be as pure as new fallen snow. Grant us a new and a right spirit, we pray. Amen.

Words of Assurance

Jesus Christ is the source of our forgiveness. He died for our sin once and for all to put to death the bonds that hold us. We are reconciled to God through Christ and made equal partners in the covenant. God is merciful and compassionate, more ready to forgive than we are to ask. Rejoice and walk in the newness of life. Amen.

Joys and Concerns of the Community

Prayers of the People

Responsive Reading

Leader: The yam is a life-sustaining symbol of African American kinship and community. Everywhere in the world where we live, we grow, cook, and eat yams. It is a symbol of our diasporic connections. Yams provide nourishment for the body as food and are used medicinally to heal the body.[20] Today, as we gather to celebrate who we are as African Americans in the universal Church, may the symbol of the yam remind us of our strong roots, our hearty constitution, our necessity to the world, and our spiritual connection to sisters and brothers everywhere. The yam was the food of our ancestors; may we remember and honor their presence in us today. The yam is food for us. Let us give thanks for this plant of the ground, which draws us together. The yam is our symbol of hope for our future generations. May we always remember our heritage as African American Christians, with pride.

Leader: What symbol do you bring?

People: (The people bring their yams, baked sweet potatoes, yam breads, pies, cookies, soups, etc. forward to the altar for blessing.)

Leader: "What is wrong, old wife? What is happening to the [people] of the yam? Seem like they just don't know how to draw up the powers from the deep like before!"[21]

People: God of the yam, Creator of all things, we pause to give you thanks for the rich soil that produced our foreparents and was our homeland. The yam reminds us that you made us tough and durable, sweet and plentiful, resilient and tender. In your divine wisdom, you have nourished us and provided us with growth opportunities in all the places of the diaspora. Our roots have held secure. Our knowledge has increased. Our community has been saved in spite of dangers, seen and unseen. Like the yam, we have grown in the deepness of your love. We have sprung forth in the proper time and become a bumper crop, willing to share our joy of abundant life. We call upon your power today.

Leader: Too often we have forgotten and neglected the power we have received from you. Too often we have believed that we were ugly and misshapen, as the yam. Many times we have despaired at our colors, as varied as the yam. And we have been misused and neglected because of our durability, like the yam. Yet the yam has endured the rigors of time and the storm-tossed travel, from shore to shore. It reminds us of our story, and we call upon your power today.

People: We bless you for the yam and the many ways it has sustained us. As a protein staple it has fed us. As a tasty side dish, it has been offered with our leafy greens. And we have delighted in sweet potato pies and breads, which are our ethnic offerings to the world. You have blessed us, a misused and neglected people, to be living symbols of your sustaining grace and care.

Leader: We call upon your power today, Holy One, for the black Church and for its founders, who uplifted our uniqueness to the wider Church and made us more aware of our sweet, sweet spirit of celebration and joy, which needed to be spread. We call upon your power.

People: Majestic Sovereign, we call upon your power. For the black Church everywhere, its leadership and direction, as we continue to walk a lonesome valley and cry out for justice and long-denied liberty, we pray.

Leader: Lavishly Generous God, we call upon your power. For the people of the yam everywhere, we lift our hearts in prayer. As we gather to rehearse our faith story and to celebrate our witness to the wider world, we need your power in order that the black Church might continue to be articulated courage, visible dignity, strong endurance, and steadfast faithfulness in our service to you.

People: Name Above All Names, we offer thanksgiving for the ability to eat from the table, which is loaded with symbols of our heritage. We bless you for knowing us and calling us by name. We bless you for the power we have from you to be valiant, strong, gentle, and grace-filled as we face the days ahead. We bless you for the yam. We are thankful for food from home, which has been a constant in our unsteady existence.

And because you have sustained the yam, we are assured that your grace will keep us and the black Church in the generations ahead.

Unison: We are proud African Americans, people of the yam. We will walk and talk with the power of God and give praise to the awesome High God always. Amen.

Hymn of Praise

"God Will Take Care of You"[22]

Scripture Lessons

The Living Word

Hymn of Response

"Remember Me"[23]

Offertory Invitation

People of the yam know what is right. We are required to love justice, to seek mercy, and to walk humbly with our God. People of the yam do what is right. We share from our resources in order that all the community might prosper. People of the yam give generously from hearts filled with thanks.

Offertory Praise

Yam Maker and Preserver, we are they who have acquired and mastered the art of stretch and make do! We appreciate your creative power at work in us today. Receive these, our offerings, and multiply them for greater use in the world.

Doxology

Benediction

Leader: You are African Americans, people of the yam, made of beautiful black, rich earth.

People: We are African Americans, people of the yam, brought by God to be witnesses and lights in the world.

Leader: You are African Americans, people of the yam, a gift to the Church and sacred to our God.

People: We are African Americans, people of the yam, and we will continue to offer who we are, for we are forever held in the loving arms of our God. Amen and amen.

Hymn of Benediction and Blessing

"We Shall Overcome"[24]

COMMUNION LITURGY[25]

Call to Worship

Leader: Sisters and brothers, everything has been made ready. The table is spread!
People: We come to meet the living God, who is beyond our intellectual comprehension and is yet as close as our breath.
Leader: Everything has been made ready. The table is spread!
People: We gather to celebrate the risen Christ, who is God with us and, nevertheless, the One to come.
Leader: Everything has been made ready! The table is spread!
People: We assemble to be revived by the life-renewing Holy Spirit, who empowers our search for shalom in this unfriendly world.
Leader: In the bread and in the wine we will receive strength for the journey.
People: Everything has been made ready. The table is spread! Thanks be to the risen Christ. Amen.

Hymn of Celebration

"All Hail the Power"[26]

Call to Confession

When we gather to praise God, we remember that we are God's people who have preferred our wills to God's. Accepting God's power to become new persons in Christ, let us confess our sin before God and one another.

Confession

Eternal God, we confess that often we have failed to be an obedient Church. We have not done your will. We have broken your laws. We have rebelled against your love. We have not loved our neighbors. We have not heard the cry of the needy. Forgive us, we pray. Free us for joyful obedience through Jesus Christ, our Lord. Amen.

Words of Assurance

Leader: Hear the good news! "Christ died for us while we were yet sinners; that is God's own proof of universal love toward us." In the name of Jesus Christ you are forgiven.

People: In the name of Jesus Christ, we are forgiven! Glory to God. Amen.

Prayers for the Community

(Response to each stanza: Sing "Kum Ba Yah.")[27]

Leader: Someone's crying today, Lord. And the cries are of millions. Hear the crying men and women, boys and girls. Capture the tears of fear and suffering, the tears of weakness and pain, the tears of brokenness and disappointment. We are crying, Lord. Transform our lives.

People: Kum Ba Yah, my Lord.

Leader: Too many are dying today, Lord. Too many die of hunger and homelessness. Too many die because of the systemic racist structures that deny the poor and enhance the rich. Too many are dying, Lord, because we neglect the power and gifts you have placed within us and told us to utilize. Too many are dying because we are not fully united in purpose and determined to stand together and be your witnesses. Too many are dying, Lord. Transform our lives.

People: Kum Ba Yah, my Lord.

Leader: Someone's praying today, Lord, even while we wait. And we join with the faithful at prayer, even with our feeble and weak voices, in our broken and halting speech, in our wrestling and struggling, trying to believe that you hear and answer our prayers. But we are someone's today, Lord, while we wait in hope. We pray you will rekindle our spirits, touch us with your love, and empower us for the journey. We are praying, Lord. Transform our lives.

People: Kum Ba Yah, my Lord.

Leader: For the healing of the nations, come by here, Lord. For the balm in Gilead that is needed for our wounded bodies and grieving spirits, come by here. For the restoration of our families, the authentic coming together of our communities, and the salvation of our souls, come by here. For your Church, fractured and splintered. For your world, divided and in chaos. For the sake of the leaders you have placed over us and for the sake of Jesus Christ, oh Lord, come by here. Amen and amen.

Pastoral Prayer

Affirmation of Faith

We believe in the God of colors: A creating God who formed us from the dust of black earth. We believe that this God came in the form of a despised minority, named Jesus. He was born of a virgin, powerless, helpless, and dependent. He was rejected and carried our shame. Without cause they hung him high, stretched him wide, and mocked him as he died. He died, at the hands of a lynch mob, for our sake. Evil did not gain the victory. For Jesus rose, victorious over sin, death, and hell. We celebrate the risen Saviour who gave his life for justice and equality of all. We join his struggle as disciples. He has come and he will come again. He knows our troubles and journeys in us, day by day. We affirm our counselor, the Holy Spirit, who is the wisdom of God. Jesus Christ is our Rock and our salvation, the Ancient of Days and the Lion of the Tribe. We know he will come again! Amen.

The Hebrew Lesson

The Gospel Lesson

Hymn of Preparation

"Emmanuel, Emmanuel"[28]

The Challenge of the Word

Hymn of Response

"Majesty, Worship His Majesty"[29]

The Peace

The table is open to all who will receive the ministry of reconciliation and pass it on. Let's offer each other signs and symbols of God's shalom.

The Great Thanksgiving

Leader: The Lord is with you.
People: And also with you.
Leader: Lift up your hearts.
People: We lift them up to the Lord.

Leader: God of our ancestors, hope of the living ones, we offer you praise and thanksgiving because you loved us enough to empty yourself of awesome divinity and entered into our human struggle, taking upon yourself our despised color and position in life. You have walked our valley of sorrow and felt the whip tear the flesh from your back. You know what it means to be denied justice and to be abandoned by friends. So when our nationality is reviled, our color scorned, and our dignity defamed until we are without comfort or hope, we remember you.

You called together twelve and worked to achieve unity. You taught self-determination and role modeled hard work and responsibility. You healed and set free in order that others might maintain their economic development and have purpose in their daily lives. You are the essence of creativity and promised that greater works we would perform. It was your faith that allowed you to march with determination up Golgatha's hill. With help from one black brother, Simon, you carried a cruel cross. And on that old, rugged cross you became our sin and shame, sanctifying pain and giving birth to the universal Church. So, with all the company of saints, those who have walked with you to Calvary, that they might be raised to new life with you, we praise you, saying:

People: Holy, holy, holy, compassionate, identifying God. Heaven and earth are full of your glory; Hosanna in the highest. Blessed is the One who comes in the name of God; Hosanna in the highest.

Leader: Blessed is our Savior, Jesus. Bone of our bone and flesh of our flesh, who the cup of suffering did not shirk; who, on the night that he was betrayed, took bread, gave thanks, broke it, and said, "This is my body, broken for you. Eat it, in remembrance of me." In the same manner, after the supper, he took the cup, gave thanks, and said: "This cup is the new covenant in my blood. It is poured out for you and for many, for the forgiveness of sin. Whenever you drink it, remember me."

People: Christ has died. Christ has risen. Christ will come again.

As we eat this bread and drink this cup, we proclaim Christ's suffering and death until he comes. In the body that is broken and the cup that is poured out we restore to memory and hope all of the unnamed and forgotten victims of blatant sins. We hunger for the bread of that new age and thirst for the wine of the realm that is to come. Come, Holy Spirit, hover over and dwell within these earthly things, and make us one body with Christ, that we, who are baptized into his death, may walk in newness of life; that what is sown in dishonor may be raised in glory, and what is sown in weakness may be raised in power. Amen.

Leader: Sisters and brothers, Christ has made everything ready. Come and eat, the table is spread.

Breaking of the Bread

Lonely stalks of wheat stood useless in a field, until they were pulled together, bruised, crushed, beaten, and baked to become bread for a hungry world. When we break this loaf, it is our sharing in the body of Christ.

Taking of the Cup

Single grapes lay close to the ground, until they were picked, stomped, crushed, and smashed to provide drink for a thirsty world. When we give thanks over the cup, it is our sharing in the blood of Christ. This is an open altar. All who name Jesus as Sovereign, to the glory of God, are welcome at this table.

Doxology

Benediction

Leader: We have gathered for community worship and feasting. Now we are sent again into the world, with the authority and power of the Holy Spirit.

People: God has prepared a table for us, in the presence of our enemies.

Leader: We require nothing else for the journey. All our needs are supplied by an all-sufficient God.

People: A mighty fortress is our God, a shelter in time of storm.

Leader: The world has not changed. Evil continues. But, we are mandated by El Shaddai to make a difference.

People: We will cry loud and spare not! We will lift up our voices like trumpets in Zion! We will proclaim that this is the day of our God. Amen and amen.

Hymn of Benediction and Blessing

"My Tribute"[30]

NOTES

1. "Mary Had a Little Lamb," traditional.
2. Rich Mullins, "Our God Is an Awesome God," © 1988 BMG Songs, Inc.
3. Ken Barker and Tom Tenke, "What a Mighty God We Serve," © 1989 Word Music.
4. Leonard E. Smith, Jr., "Our God Reigns," © 1978 New Jerusalem Music.
5. John W. Work, Jr. "Go! Tell It on the Mountain," 1907.
6. "Kum Ba Yah (Come by Here)," African American spiritual.
7. Margaret Pleasant Douraux, "What Shall I Render?" 1975.
8. Smith, "Our God Reigns."
9. "Ain't Dat Good News?" traditional.
10. Isaac Watts, "Joy to the World." 1719.
11. "Take Me to the Water," African American spiritual.
12. Charles Wesley/George Elderkin, "Jesus Is the Light of the World."
13. Fanny J. Crosby, "Jesus, Keep Me Near the Cross," 1869.
14. "Blessed Be the Name of the Lord," USA camp meeting chorus (Psalm 72:19), melody arranged by Ralph E. Hudson, 1887.
15. "Take Me to the Water," African American spiritual.
16. Inspiration for this service was provided by Ms. Deborah Tinsley Taylor, a poet-singer-minister-sister-friend, from the Northern Illinois Conference/UMC.
17. Cain Hope Felder, *Stony is the Road We Trod* (Minneapolis: Fortress Press, 1991).
18. James Weldon Johnson, "Lift Every Voice and Sing," © 1921 Edward B. Marks Music Co.: renewed.
19. Adapted from *United Methodist Book of Worship* (Nashville: United Methodist Publishing House, 1992).
20. bell hooks, *Sisters of the Yam: Black Women and Self-Recovery* (Boston South End Press, 1993), 13.
21. Ibid.
22. Civilla D. Martin, "God Will Take Care of You," 1904.
23. "Remember Me," traditional.
24. "We Shall Overcome," African American spiritual.
25. Adapted from communion liturgies in *United Methodist Book of Worship* (Nashville: United Methodist Publishing House, 1992).
26. Edward Perronet, "All Hail the Power of Jesus' Name," 1779; alt. by John Rippon, 1787.
27. "Kum Ba Yah (Come by Here)," African American spiritual.
28. Bob McGee, "Emmanuel, Emmanuel," © 1976 C. A. Music (div. of Christian Artists Corp.).
29. Jack Hayford, "Majesty, Worship His Majesty," © 1981 Rocksmith Music c/o Trust Music Management.
30. Andraé Crouch, "My Tribute," © 1971 Communiqué Music, Inc.